SPIRITUAL
PROVOKING

SPIRITUAL
&
THOUGHT-PROVOKING
QUOTATIONS

DES MACHALE

MERCIER PRESS

MERCIER PRESS
PO Box 5, 5 French Church Street, Cork
and
16 Hume Street, Dublin

Trade enquiries to CMD DISTRIBUTION,
55a Spruce Avenue, Stillorgan Industrial Park, Blackrock, Dublin

© Des MacHale 1997

A CIP is available for this book from the British Library

ISBN 1 85635 169 6

10 9 8 7 6 5 4 3 2 1

DEDICATED TO
BRIDIE AND MICHAEL WITH MUCH LOVE

Printed in Ireland by Colour Books Ltd.

Contents

INTRODUCTION

For many years I have been reading and hearing hundreds of quotes that made me feel 'Wow, that one absolutely hits the spot' or 'that's a true or a deep or a profound saying'. It takes a great deal of skill and wisdom to distil a sermon, a piece of philosophy or a telling truth into twenty words or less, but that is what all the people quoted in this book have managed to do.

The quotes that I have chosen come from both men and women, old and young, famous and infamous, rich and poor, learned and unlearned – indeed all human life is here. However, they have all got one thing in common – they are spiritual in the widest possible sense of that word. This does not mean they are religious, though religion has by no means been excluded. I do not always agree with the sentiments they express and I am sure that neither will the reader, but they are well put and deserve a hearing.

After compiling this collection and therefore reading through it many times I feel that these quotes are uplifting. They make me aspire to higher things, they make me want to become a better person and become more sympathetic to those round about me. They fill me with idealism but at times sadness also, and not a few of them bring a lump to my throat and a tear to my eye.

When taking medication we are often instructed to take three tablets per day – one in the morning, one in the afternoon and one in the evening. May I exhort the reader to partake of this book in the same way? Take three quotes each day and contemplate these and these only – the book will thus last you over a year (excellent value!) and it has the potential to change your life by listening to the collected wisdom of the ages from the Ancient Greeks right down to present-day sages.

Wisdom is benign and as wise men and women speak to us from the past we feel that they are in sympathy with us and have had very similar experiences. Despite huge changes in living conditions and science and technology, human nature and human problems have changed very little over the past three thousand years. There are many millions of people on this planet who are in need of advice, encouragement and hope. If this book succeeds in helping even one such person then it will have served its purpose.

DES MACHALE

1: LIFE AND DEATH

1:1　Not a shred of evidence exists in favour of the idea that life is serious.

Brendan Gill

1:2　Life is like a B-grade movie. You don't want to leave in the middle of it, but you don't want to see it again either.

Ted Turner

1:3　Executing the guilty is a deterrent to crime for that one person only.

Benjamin Coats

1:4　The fallen – age shall not weary them, nor the years condemn. At the going down of the sun and in the morning, we will remember them.

Laurence Binyon

1:5　Old age is an island surrounded by death.

Juan Montalvo

1:6　'Leave the dead to bury their dead'. There is not a single word of Christ to which the Christian religion has paid less attention.

André Gide

1:7　Life is not a dress rehearsal.

Paul Hogan

1:8　Passionate grief does not link us with the dead, but cuts us off from them.

C. S. Lewis

1:9　If we do not live now, when do we begin?

J. B. Priestley

1:10　I should like to abolish funerals; the time to mourn a person is at his birth, not his death.

Montesquieu

1:11 Life can be understood only backwards; but it must be lived forwards.

Sören Kierkegaard

1:12 Men fear death as children fear to go in the dark; and as that natural fear in children is increased by tales, so is the other.

Francis Bacon

1:13 Anyone who makes a lot of money quickly must be pretty crooked – honest pushing away at the grindstone never made anyone a bomb.

Marilyn Rice-Davies

1:14 It is said that sheep may get lost simply by nibbling away at the grass and never looking up. That can be true for any of us. We can focus so much on what is immediately before us that we fail to see life in larger perspective.

Donald Bitsberger

1:15 The living are the dead on holiday.

Maurice Maeterlinck

1:16 What we call mourning for our dead is perhaps not so much grief at not being able to call them back as it is grief at not being able to want to do so.

Thomas Mann

1:17 Death is the only solution of the problem of life which has not so far definitely proved to be the wrong one.

Raymond Asquith

1:18 It is because everything must come to an end that everything is so beautiful.

Charles Ramuz

1:19 The first breath is the beginning of death.

Thomas Fuller

1:20 In suicide, as in no other cause of death, the true victims are the ones who must live on after a loved one commits this selfish act.

Colleen Mastroianni

1:21 The tyrant dies and his rule is over; the martyr dies and his rule begins.

Sören Kierkegaard

1:22 Most people die at the last minute; others twenty years beforehand, some even earlier. They are the wretched of the earth.

Louis Céline

1:23 Death is the night of this turbulent day that we call life.

Bernadin de St Pierre

1:24 Death is the stake one puts up in order to play the game of life.

Jean Giraudoux

1:25 The thought of suicide is a powerful comfort; it helps one through many a dreadful night.

Friedrich Nietzsche

1:26 Only two things are certain in this world – death and ingratitude.

Denis Hamilton

1:27 Life is a series of crises separated by brief periods of self-delusion.

Richard Rosen

1:28 You are here only for a short visit. Don't hurry, don't worry. And be sure to smell the flowers along the way.

Walter Hagen

1:29 If I had known that death would be this easy, I wouldn't have worried about it.

Bobby Jones

1:30 To live a long life, acquire an incurable ailment in your youth.

James Gibbons

1:31 It is better to live rich than to die rich.

Samuel Johnson

1:32 Let us endeavour so to live that when we come to die even the undertaker will be sorry.

Mark Twain

1:33 I think I will not hang myself today.

G. K. Chesterton

1:34 The crash of the whole solar and stellar systems could kill you only once.

Thomas Carlyle

1:35 There are few things easier than to live badly and die well.

Oscar Wilde

1:36 Life is mostly froth and bubble;
    Two things stand like stone,
    Kindness in another's trouble
    Courage in your own.

Adam Gordon

1:37 Respect for the fragility and importance of an individual life is still the first mark of an educated man.

Norman Cousins

1:38 Living is a disease from which sleep gives us relief eight hours a day.

Nicolas Chamfort

1:39 We are afraid of death because we are all doing it for the first time.

Gwen Davies

1:40 If some died and others did not, death would be a terrible affliction.

Jean De La Bruyère

1:41 Life consists not in holding good cards, but in playing well those you do hold.

Josh Billings

1:42 Courage is almost a contradiction in terms: it means a strong desire to live taking the form of a readiness to die.

G. K. Chesterton

1:43 Many people who spend their time mourning over the brevity of life could make it seem longer if they did a little more work.

Don Marquis

1:44 By the time a man is ready to die, he is fit to live.

Edgar Howe

1:45 Life is perhaps most widely regarded as a bad dream between two awakenings and every day is a life in miniature.

Eugene O'Neill

1:46 When we execute a murderer, we probably make the same mistake as the child who strikes a chair it has bumped into.

G. C. Lichtenberg

1:47 Why are we so fond of life that begins with a cry and ends with a groan?

Mary Warwick

1:48 More people die in the United States of too much food than of too little food.

J. K. Galbraith

1:49 Nobody on his deathbed ever said 'I wish I had spent more time on my job'.

Paul Tsongas

1:50 There is nothing terrible in life for the man who realises there is nothing terrible in death.

Epicurus

1:51 Every parting gives a foretaste of death; every coming togeth-er again a foretaste of the resurrection. This is why even people who were indifferent to each other rejoice so much if they come together again after twenty or thirty years separation.

Arthur Schopenhauer

1:52 Death is certain – life is not.

Junior Blair

1:53 Each man's life is a labyrinth at the centre of which lies his death and even after his death it may be that he passes through a final maze before it is all ended for him. Within the great maze of a man's life are many smaller ones, each seemingly complete in itself, and in passing through each one he dies in part, for in each he leaves behind him a part of his life and it lies dead behind him. It is a para-dox of the labyrinth that its centre appears to be the way to freedom.

Michael Ayrton

1:54 The meaning of life is that it stops.

Franz Kafka

1:55 Death is the cure for all diseases.

Thomas Browne

1:56 It's a funny thing about life: if you refuse to accept anything but the very best you will very often get it.

Somerset Maugham

1:57 That which does not kill us, makes us stronger.

Friedrich Nietzsche

1:58 To himself everyone is immortal; he may know that he is going to die, but he can never know that he is dead.

Samuel Butler

1:59 Fundamentally, all writing is about the same thing: it's about dying, about the brief flicker of time we have here, and the frustrations that it creates.

Mordecai Richler

1:60 Man is ready to die for an idea, provided that idea is not quite clear to him.

Paul Eldridge

1:61 The reason so many people never get anywhere in life is because, when opportunity knocks, they are out in the backyard looking for four-leaf clovers.

Walter Chrysler

2: GOD AND SATAN

2:1   God is subtle, but He is not malicious.

Albert Einstein

2:2   Those who set out to serve both God and Mammon soon discover that there is no God.

Logan P. Smith

2:3   The hottest places in hell are reserved for those who, in a period of moral crisis, maintain their neutrality.

Dante

2:4   No man can ever enter heaven until he is first convinced he deserves hell.

John W. Everett

2:5   I believe Satan to exist for two reasons; first the Bible says so; and second, I've done business with him.

Dwight L. Moody

2:6   Glory be to God, who determined, for reasons we know not, that wickedness and stupidity should rule the world.

Arthur de Gobineau

2:7   Aim at heaven and you will get earth thrown in. Aim at earth and you will get neither.

C. S. Lewis

2:8   When men grow virtuous in their old age they make a sacrifice to God of only the devil's leavings.

Alexander Pope

2:9   Sour godliness is the devil's religion.

John Wesley

2:10 Let us not be too hasty in judging the Devil. It must be remembered that we have heard only one side of the case; God has written all the books.

Samuel Butler

2:11 'My country, right or wrong' is an insult hurled at God.

Jerome K. Jerome

2:12 Has this world been so kind to you that you should leave it with regret? There are better things ahead than any we leave behind.

C. S. Lewis

2:13 Do not ask God the way to heaven; He will show you the hardest way.

Stanislaw Lec

2:14 Thou hast created us after Thyself, O God, and our hearts are restless till they rest in Thee.

St Augustine

2:15 The condition upon which God hath given liberty to man is eternal vigilance.

John Philpot Curran

2:16 Of all political ideas, perhaps the most dangerous is the wish to make people perfect and happy. The attempt to realise heaven on earth has always produced a hell.

Karl Popper

2:17 When I wrote the 'Hallelujah Chorus', I thought I did see all Heaven before me, and the Great God Himself.

G. F. Handel

2:18 I did not write *Uncle Tom's Cabin*. God wrote it. I merely took His dictation.

Harriet Beecher Stowe

2:19 I expect to pass through this world but once; any good thing therefore that I can do, or any kindness that I can show to any fellow creature, let me do it now; let me not defer or neglect it, for I shall not pass this way again.

Stephen Grellet

2:20 Although God demands a whole heart, He will accept a broken one if He gets all the pieces.

Mary Irving

2:21 Maybe this world is just another planet's hell.

Aldous Huxley

2:22 The test of a man or woman's breeding is how they behave in a quarrel.

George Bernard Shaw

2:23 God has no need of puppets. He pays men the compliment of allowing them to live without Him if they choose. But if they live without Him in this life, they must also live without Him in the next.

Leon Morris

2:24 Thousands have gone to heaven who have never read one page of the Bible.

Francis A. Baker

2:25 I tremble for my country when I reflect that God is just.

Thomas Jefferson

2:26 It takes a long while for a naturally trustful person to reconcile himself to the idea that after all God will not help him.

H. L. Mencken

2:27 Lucifer is the patron saint of the visual arts. Colour, form – all these are the work of Lucifer.

Kenneth Anger

2:28 There but for the grace of God go I.

John Bradford

2:29 Business underlies everything in our natural life, including our spiritual life. Witness the fact that in the Lord's Prayer the first petition is for daily bread. No one can worship God or love his neighbour on an empty stomach.

Woodrow Wilson

2:30 God is not dead, but neither is Satan.

C. A. Risley

2:31 There is no such thing as 'safe' sex. Handing out condoms to teenagers is like issuing them with water pistols for a raging inferno.

Robert Noble

2:32 God gives talent; work transforms it into genius.

Anna Pavlova

2:33 The common man, who doesn't know what to do with this life, wants another which shall be endless.

Anatole France

2:34 You shall have joy or you shall have power, said God; you shall not have both.

Ralph W. Emerson

2:35 I sometimes think that God, in creating man, somewhat overestimated his ability.

Oscar Wilde

2:36 The devil divides the world between atheism and superstition.

George Herbert

2:37 I have always kept one end in view, namely, with all good will to conduct a well-regulated church music to the honour of God.

J. S. Bach

2:38 I am not afraid that God will destroy the world, but I am afraid that He may abandon it to wander blindly in the sophisticated wasteland of contemporary civilisation.

Carlo Carretto

2:39 God never gives a cross to bear larger than we can carry.

Rose Kennedy

2:40 There is only one thing God cannot do – He cannot please everybody.

Brian Cavanaugh

2:41 Man creates God in his own image.

Ernst Haeckel

2:42 Our time in this world is not the whole story of our existence. Men must always believe this, have believed this, will always believe it in one form or other.

Malcolm Muggeridge

2:43 Heaven and hell are one place and we all go there: to those who are prepared, it is heaven; to those who are not, it is hell.

Lincoln Steffens

2:44 There is no God, but Mary is His mother.

William James

2:45 Light (God's eldest daughter) is a principal beauty in building.

Thomas Fuller

2:46 The devil does not tempt unbelievers and sinners who are already his own.

Thomas à Kempis

2:47 The next time the devil reminds you of your past, remind him of his future.

C. S. Lewis

2:48 Pain is God's megaphone to rouse a dead world.

C. S. Lewis

2:49 Better to rule in Hell than to serve in Heaven.

John Milton

2:50 God seems to have left the receiver off the hook, and time is running out.

Arthur Koestler

2:51 The Lord never spoke of success. He spoke only of faithfulness in love. That is the only success that really counts.

Mother Teresa

2:52 And I said to the man who stood at the gate of the year 'Give me a light that I may tread safely into the unknown'. And he replied 'Go out into the darkness and put your hand into the hand of God. That shall be to you better than light and safer than a known way'.

Minnie L. Haskins

2:53 No paradise is complete without its snake.

Edith Howie

2:54 You'll never get to be a saint if you deny the bit of the devil in you.

Ellis Peters

2:55 God comprehends even the atheism of the atheist.

Mahatma Gandhi

2:56 One cannot walk through a mass-production factory and not feel that one is in Hell.

W. H. Auden

2:57 The doctor is an enemy of God: he battles against death.

William Ostler

2:58 I cannot imagine how the clockwork of the universe can exist without a clockmaker.

Voltaire

2:59 Beware of the man whose God is in the skies.

George Bernard Shaw

2:60 Every man is his own law court and punishes himself enough.

Patricia Highsmith

2:61 If I find in myself a desire which no experience in this world can satisfy, the most probable explanation is that I was made for another world.

C. S. Lewis

2:62 To a man with an empty stomach, food is God.

Mahatma Gandhi

2:63 Confusion evolves into order spontaneously. What God really said was 'Let there be chaos'.

Rosario Levins

2:64 A God who let us prove His existence would be an idol.

Dietrich Bonhoeffer

2:65 I am a great and sublime fool. But then I am God's fool, and all His work must be contemplated with respect.

Mark Twain

2:66 Perhaps God is not dead; perhaps God is Himself mad.

R. D. Laing

2:67 God designed the stomach to eject what is bad for it, but not the human brain.

Konrad Adenauer

2:68 If there is no God, it is up to man to be as moral as he can.

Steve Allen

2:69 We know God will forgive us our sins, but what will He think of our virtues?

Peter de Vries

3: HUMAN BEHAVIOUR

3:1   Sooner or later everyone sits down to a banquet of consequences.

Frank Gannon

3:2   If we had no winter, the spring would not be so pleasant; if we did not sometimes taste of adversity, prosperity would not be so welcome.

Anne Bradstreet

3:3   Resolved: never to do anything which I should be afraid to do if it were the last hour of my life.

Jonathan Edwards

3:4   If you had only six months to live, what would you do, and if you're not doing that now, why not?

Stephen Thomas

3:5   No man is an island, entire of itself; every man is a piece of the Continent, a part of the main. Any man's death diminishes me, because I am involved in mankind; therefore never send to know for whom the bell tolls, it tolls for thee.

John Donne

3:6   I put the question directly to myself: 'Suppose that all your objects in life were realised; that all the changes in institutions and opinions which you are looking forward to could be completely effected at this very instant: would this be a great joy and happiness to you? And an irrepressible self-consciousness distinctly answered 'No!'

John Stuart Mill

3:7   You can fill a twelve-quart bucket with water and pour it into a wicker basket, fill the bucket again and pour it in again, and keep doing it all day long. You will never fill the basket; but I'll tell you one thing: at the end of the day you will have a clean basket.

Roy Gustafson

3:8   If we are to abolish the death penalty, I should like to see the first steps taken by our friends the murderers.

Alphonse Kerr

3:9   To enjoy freedom we have to control ourselves.

Virginia Woolf

3:10   Tough times don't last, tough people do.

Robert Schuller

3:11   No people do so much harm as those who go about doing good.

Mandell Creighton

3:12   A large part of altruism, even when it is perfectly honest, is grounded upon the fact that it is uncomfortable to have unhappy people about one.

H. L. Mencken

3:13   Our business in the world is not to succeed, but to continue to fail in good spirits.

Robert Louis Stevenson

3:14   Nothing arouses ambition so much in the heart as the trumpet clang of another's fame.

Baltasar Gracian

3:15   Do not buy what you want, but what you need; what you do not need is dear at a farthing.

Marcus Cato

3:16   He who is content with nothing possesses all things.

Nicholas Boileau

3:17   Liberty too can corrupt, and absolute liberty can corrupt absolutely.

Gertrude Himmelfarls

3:18   In grave difficulties and where there is little hope, the boldest measures are the safest.

Livy

3:19   How wise are thy commandments, Lord. Each of them applies to somebody I know.

Sam Levenson

3:20   If two men on the same job agree all the time, then one is useless. If they disagree all the time, then both are useless.

Darryl Zanuck

3:21   The man who first abused his fellows with swear-words instead of bashing their brains out with a club, should be counted among those who laid the foundations of civilisation.

John Cohen

3:22   Charity that is always beginning at home stays there.

Austin O'Malley

3:23   I cannot give you the formula for success, but I can give you the formula for failure. Try to please everybody.

Herbert B. Swope

3:24   True generosity consists precisely in fighting to destroy the causes which nourish false charity.

Paulo Freire

3:25   The first person who, having enclosed a piece of ground said 'This is mine', and found people simple enough to believe him, was the real founder of civil society.

J. J. Rousseau

3:26   When we talk so confidently of liberty, we are unaware of the awful servitude of poverty when means are so small that there is literally no choice.

Barbara Ward

3:27   Nothing will ever be attempted if all possible objections must first be overcome.

Samuel Johnson

3:28   Leave the beaten track occasionally and dive into the woods. You will be certain to find something you have never seen before.

Alexander Graham Bell

3:29   A long dispute means that both parties are wrong.

Bob Phillips

3:30   Anyone who has lived his life to the fullest extent has a scandal buried somewhere. And anybody who doesn't, I have no interest in meeting. You show me somebody who has led a perfect life and I'll show you a dullard.

Rob Lowe

3:31   To keep a lamp burning we have to keep putting oil in it.

Mother Teresa

3:32   He who praises everybody, praises nobody.

Samuel Johnson

3:33   One great strong unselfish soul in every community could actually redeem the world.

Eugene P. Bertin

3:34   In the whole history of law and order, the biggest step was taken by primitive man when the tribe sat in a circle and allowed only one man to speak at a time. An accused who is shouted down has no rights whatever.

Curtis Bok

3:35   The worst thing I ever said to an umpire was 'are you sure?'

Rod Laver

3:36   No steam or gas drives anything until it is confined. No life ever grows great until it is focused, dedicated, disciplined.

Harry E. Fosdick

3:37　Aim at perfection in everything, though in most things it is unattainable. However, they who aim at it and persevere will come much nearer to it than those whose laziness and despondency make them give it up as unattainable.

Lord Chesterfield

3:38　He that has a secret should not only hide it, but hide that he has it to hide.

Thomas Carlyle

3:39　The world is for the most part, a collective madhouse, and practically everyone, however 'normal' his facade, is faking sanity.

John Astin

3:40　You can get through life with bad manners – but it's easier with good manners.

Lillian Gish

3:41　Kindness is a language which the deaf can hear and the blind can read.

Mark Twain

3:42　Constraints are not necessarily negative. They may force you to try avenues you would otherwise have ignored.

Caesar Pelli

3:43　You will rest from vain fancies if you perform every act in life as though it were your last.

Marcus Aurelius

3:44　The way to succeed is to double your failure rate.

Thomas Edison

3:45　When you get into a tight place and everything goes against you, until it seems you could not hold on a minute longer, never give up then, for that is just the place and time that the tide will turn.

Harriet Beecher Stowe

3:46 Experience is the name people give to their mistakes.

Oscar Wilde

3:47 Blessed is the person who is too busy to worry in the daytime, and too sleepy to worry at night.

Leo Ackman

3:48 One of the deadliest things on earth is a cheerful person with no sense of humour.

G. K. Chesterton

3:49 I long to accomplish a great and noble task, but it is my chief duty to accomplish humble tasks as though they were great and noble. The world is moved along, not only by the mighty shoves of its heroes, but also by the aggregate of the tiny pushes of each honest worker.

Helen Keller

3:50 Good breeding consists in concealing how much we think of ourselves and how little we think of the other person.

Mark Twain

3:51 Strong people make as many and as ghastly mistakes as weak people. The difference is that strong people admit them, laugh at them, learn from them. That is how they became strong.

Richard Needham

3:52 There is always another chance. This thing we call 'failure' is not the falling down but the staying down.

Mary Pickford

3:53 To practice what we preach is rightly expected, but to preach what we practice would be to invite suspicion.

Arnold Haller

3:54 You can sign a thousand autographs, but walk away with two or three left stranded and you are branded as too big and rich to bother with the common man.

Fred Couples

3:55   No one gossips about other people's secret virtues.

Bertrand Russell

3:56   Where is human nature so weak as in a bookstore?

Henry Ward Beecher

3:57   Three may keep a secret if two of them are dead.

Benjamin Franklin

3:58   No great achievement is possible without persistent work.

Bertrand Russell

3:59   Sanity is madness put to good uses.

George Santayana

3:60   Never cut what you can untie.

Joseph Joubert

3:61   Great men never complain about lack of time.

Fred Smith

3:62   There is hardly anything in the world that some man cannot make a little worse and sell a little cheaper, and the people who consider price only are this man's lawful prey.

John Ruskin

3:63   Nothing is illegal if a hundred businessmen decide to do it.

Andrew Young

3:64   Every American crusade winds up as a racket.

John P. Roche

3:65   The absurd person is the one who never changes.

Auguste Barthélémy

3:66   Millionaires seldom laugh.

Andrew Carnegie

3:67   We must interpret a bad temper as a sign of inferiority.

Alfred Adler

3:68   All man's troubles come from not knowing how to sit still in one room.

Blaise Pascal

3:69   Five thousand years ago what I am saying was right. In five thousand years time what I am saying will still be right: cleanliness, honesty, decency, respect for other people, politeness, good manners, integrity – they will never be old-fashioned.

Charles Forte

3:70   Since when do you have to agree with people to defend them from injustice?

Lillian Hellman

3:71   Wild animals never kill for sport. Man is the only one to whom the torture and death of his fellow creatures is amusing in itself.

James A. Froude

3:72   What one has to do usually can be done.

Eleanor Roosevelt

3:73   Remember, no one can make you feel inferior without your consent.

Eleanor Roosevelt

3:74   The mass of men lead lives of quiet desperation.

Henry D. Thoreau

3:75   Riches do not consist in the possession of treasures but in the use made of them.

Napoleon Bonaparte

3:76   Boxing is as cruel a blood sport as hunting; although the victims aren't dumb animals but poor blacks.

Michael Arditti

3:77   If you can play as if it means nothing when it means everything, then you are hard to beat.

Steve Davis

3:78 Take a rest; a field that has rested gives a beautiful crop.
Ovid

3:79 Where large sums of money are involved, it is advisable to trust nobody.
Agatha Christie

3:80 The test of a vocation is the love of the drudgery it involves.
Logan P. Smith

3:81 Hypocrisy is a sort of homage that vice pays virtue.
Thomas Fuller

3:82 Laws are spider webs through which the big flies pass and the little ones get caught.
Honoré de Balzac

3:83 Facing the press is more difficult than bathing a leper.
Mother Teresa

3:84 No innocent man buys a gun and no happy man writes his memoirs.
Raymond Payne

3:85 Gluttony is an emotional escape, a sign something is eating us.
Peter de Vries

3:86 I've had a few arguments with people, but I never bear a grudge. You know why? While you're bearing a grudge, they're out dancing.
Buddy Hackett

3:87 Perhaps the straight and narrow path would be wider if more people used it.
Kay Ingram

3:88 The reasonable man adapts himself to the world, but the unreasonable man tries to adapt the world to him. Therefore, all progress depends on the unreasonable man.
Samuel Butler

3:89   Nobody ever had to call a penalty for rules violation on me
       – I'd call it on myself.

Ben Hogan

3:90   Put all your eggs in one basket – and watch that basket.

Mark Twain

3:91   Gardens are not made by singing 'Oh how beautiful,' and
       sitting in the shade.

Rudyard Kipling

3:92   If all mankind were suddenly to practise honesty, many
       thousands of people would be sure to starve.

G. C. Lichtenberg

3:93   Four hugs a day are necessary for survival, eight for main-
       tenance, and twelve for growth.

Virginia Satir

3:94   I have never kept anything in life without wishing I had
       given it away or given anything away without wishing I
       had kept it.

Louise Brooks

3:95   One of the first principles of perseverance is to know when
       to stop persevering.

Carolyn Wells

3:96   When I was young I observed that nine out of every ten
       things I did were failures, so I did ten times more work.

George Bernard Shaw

3:97   Doing just the opposite is also a form of imitation.

G. C. Lichtenberg

3:98   I don't know of anyone who wished on his deathbed that
       he had spent more time at the office.

Peter Lynch

3:99   The only argument against an east wind is to put on your
       overcoat.

James Lowell

3:100   Eighty per cent of success is just showing up.

Woody Allen

3:101   Do what makes you anxious; don't do what makes you depressed.

James L. Collier

3:102   He who is afraid of every nettle should not piss in the grass.
Thomas Fuller

3:103   Beggars should be abolished – it is irritating to give to them and it is irritating not to.

Friedrich Nietzsche

3:104   White lies by frequent use become black ones.

Douglas Jerrold

3:105   Good resolutions are simply cheques that men draw on a bank where they have no account.

Oscar Wilde

3:106   Everyone is a moon and has a dark side which he never shows to anybody.

Mark Twain

3:107   If a man can remember what he worried about last week, he has a very good memory.

Woody Allen

3:108   A person reveals his character by nothing so clearly as the joke he resents.

G. C. Lichtenberg

3:109   Never confuse a single mistake with a final mistake.
F. Scott Fitzgerald

3:110   Don't play for safety – it's the most dangerous thing in the world.

Hugh Walpole

3:111 Laziness travels so slowly that poverty soon overtakes him.
Benjamin Franklin

3:112 Don't be afraid to take a big step if one is indicated; you can't cross a chasm in two small jumps.
David Lloyd-George

3:113 If you are going to be cheap, do not be cheap with the seed.
Jack Exum

3:114 The winds and the waves are always on the side of the ablest navigators.
Edward Gibbon

3:115 I have said it again and again: 'Everyone who preached free love in the 1960s is responsible for AIDS! And we must accept moral responsibility for it. The idea that it is an accident, a historical accident, a microbe that sort of fell from the heavens – absurd. We must face what we did.
Camilla Paglia

3:116 We tell lies when we are afraid; afraid of what we don't know, afraid of what others will think, afraid of what will be found out about us. But every time we tell a lie, the thing that we fear grows stronger.
Tad Williams

3:117 Man is a complex thing: he makes deserts bloom and lakes die.
Gil Stern

3:118 Blessed are those who can give without remembering, and take without forgetting.
Elizabeth Bibesco

3:119 Next to knowing when to seize an opportunity, the most important thing in life is to know when to forgo an advantage.
Benjamin Disraeli

3:120 I can pardon everyone's mistakes but my own.

Marcus Cato

3:121 The best way to get a bad law repealed is to enforce it strictly.

Abraham Lincoln

3:122 It is the most guilty bastard in the crowd who casts the first stone.

William McIlvanney

3:123 I have found men more kind than I expected, and less just.

Samuel Johnson

3:124 If you hoe where there are no weeds then there will be no weeds.

Michael Z. Lewin

3:125 Although there exist many thousand subjects for elegant conversation, there are persons who cannot meet a cripple without talking about feet.

Ernest Bramah

3:126 A hole in the ice is dangerous only to those who go skating.

Rex Stout

3:127 The most difficult instrument to play in the orchestra is second fiddle. I can get plenty of first violinists, but to find someone who can play second fiddle with enthusiasm – that's the problem. Yet, if there is no one to play second fiddle, there is no harmony.

Leonard Bernstein

3:128 Most people sell their souls and live with a good conscience on the proceeds.

Logan P. Smith

3:129 Most of the important things in the world have been accomplished by people who have kept on trying when there seemed to be no hope at all.

Dale Carnegie

3:130 Every obnoxious act is a cry for help.

Zig Ziglar

3:131 Never stand begging for what you have the power to earn.

Miguel de Cervantes

3:132 The best preparation for tomorrow is to do today's work superbly well.

William Ostler

3:133 Don't be afraid to give your best to what are seemingly small jobs. Every time you conquer one it makes you that much stronger. If you do the little jobs well, the big ones will tend to take care of themselves.

Dale Carnegie

3:134 It is often pleasant to stone a martyr, no matter how much we admire him.

John Barth

3:135 It is by sitting down to write every morning that one becomes a writer. Those who do not do this remain amateurs.

Gerald Brennan

3:136 When a dog runs at you, whistle for him.

Henry David Thoreau

3:137 I try. I fail. I try again. I fail better.

Samuel Beckett

3:138 People often feed the hungry so that nothing may disturb their own enjoyment of a good meal.

Somerset Maugham

3:139 How far you go in life depends on your being tender with the young, compassionate with the aged, sympathetic with the striving, and tolerant of the weak and strong. Because sometime in your life you will have been all of these.

George Carver

3:140 If you cannot win, make the fellow in front of you break the record.

Desmond Cleary

3:141 Clever liars give details but the cleverest don't.

H. L. Mencken

3:142 I found that the men and women who got to the top were those who did the jobs they had in hand, with everything they had of energy and enthusiasm and hard work.

Harry S. Truman

3:143 Ninety-nine percent of success is built on former failure.

Charles Kettering

3:144 I never knew an early-rising, hardworking, prudent man, careful of his earnings and strictly honest, who complained of bad luck.

Joseph Addison

3:145 People forget how fast you did a job – but they remember how well you did it.

Howard Newton

3:146 It is not wise to violate the rules until you know how to observe them.

T. S. Eliot

3:147 Don't ever take a fence down until you know the reason why it was put up.

G. K. Chesterton

3:148 Advertising is legalised lying.

H. G. Wells

4: ADDICTIONS AND OBSESSIONS

4:1   Addiction is an increasing desire for an act which gives less and less satisfaction.

Aldous Huxley

4:2   Every form of addiction is bad, no matter whether the narcotic be alcohol or morphine or idealism.

C. G. Jung

4:3   Alcoholism isn't a spectator sport. Eventually the whole family gets to play.

Joyce Roberta-Burdett

4:4   No one, ever, wrote anything as well after even one drink as he would have done without it.

Ring Lardner

4:5   The cat, having sat upon a hot stove lid, will not sit upon a hot stove lid again. Nor upon a cold stove lid.

Mark Twain

4:6   Abstinence is as easy to me as temperance would be difficult.

Samuel Johnson

4:7   You don't gamble to win. You gamble so you can gamble the next day.

Bert Ambrose

4:8   A drunk is a person who could stop drinking if only he would. An alcoholic is a person who would stop drinking if only he could.

Tom Shipp

4:9   One of the disadvantages of wine is that it makes a man mistake words for thoughts.

Samuel Johnson

4:10 Time spent in a casino is time given to death, a foretaste of the hour when one's flesh will be diverted to the purposes of the worm and not the will.

Rebecca West

4:11 Don't try to drown your sorrows in alcohol because sorrow is an expert swimmer.

Ann Landers

4:12 While millions have regretted tasting alcohol, no person will ever be sorry he rejected it.

Gordon Chilvers

4:13 After a certain point, money is meaningless. It ceases to be the goal. The game is what counts.

Aristotle Onassis

4:14 He who wishes to be rich in a day will be hanged in a day.

Leonardo da Vinci

4:15 We are drowning our youngsters in violence, cynicism and sadism piped into the living-room and even the nursery. The grandchildren of the kids who used to weep because the little Matchgirl froze to death now feel cheated if she isn't slugged, raped and thrown into a Bessemer converter.

Jenkin L. Jones

4:16 The sight of a drunkard is a better sermon against that vice than the best that was ever preached on that subject.

Horatio Saville

4:17 Money brings some happiness but after a certain point it just brings more money.

Neil Simon

4:18 The wish to hurt, the momentary intoxication with pain, is the loophole through which the pervert climbs into the minds of ordinary men.

Jacob Bronowski

4:19 All isms end in fascism.

Gilbert Adair

4:20 I have enough work to make me rich beyond my wildest dreams. But I've met many millionaires and they've all been miserable.

Tom Keating

4:21 A credit card is an anaesthetic which simply delays the pain.

Helen Mason

4:22 When you have found out the prevailing passion of any man, remember never to trust him as far as that passion is concerned.

Lord Chesterfield

4:23 The worst drug of today is not smack or pot – it's refined sugar.

George Hamilton

4:24 No man is smart enough to be funny when he is drunk.

Edgar Howe

4:25 You can have too much champagne to drink, but you can never have enough.

Elmer Rice

4:26 When I played drunks I had to remain sober because I did not know how to play them when I was drunk.

Richard Burton

4:27 First you take a drink, then the drink takes a drink, then the drink takes you.

F. Scott Fitzgerald

4:28 Love is a drug. It distorts reality, and that's the point of it. It would be impossible to fall in love with someone that you really saw as they are.

Fran Lebowitz

4:29 I like whiskey, I always have, and that's why I never drink it.
                                                        Robert E. Lee

4:30 I am more afraid of alcohol than of all the bullets of the enemy.
                                                        Stonewall Jackson

4:31 Fanaticism is just one step away from barbarism.
                                                        Denis Diderot

4:32 As a cure for worrying, work is better than whiskey.
                                                        Thomas Edison

4:33 All writers are vain, selfish and lazy, and at the very bottom of their motives there lies a mystery. Writing a book is a horrible exhausting struggle, like a long bout of some painful illness. One would never undertake such a thing if one were not driven on by some demon whom one can neither resist nor understand. For all one knows that demon is simply the same instinct that makes a baby squall for attention.
                                                        George Orwell

5: YOUTH AND AGE

5:1   We are fighting abortion by adoption. We have sent word to the clinics, to the hospitals, to the police stations. Please do not destroy the child. We will take the child.

Mother Teresa

5:2   Youth is a malady of which one becomes cured a little every day.

Benito Mussolini

5:3   No one is so old that he cannot live another year, or so young that he cannot die today.

Fernando de Rojas

5:4   Generally young men are regarded as radicals. This is a popular misconception. The most conservative persons I ever met are college undergraduates.

Woodrow Wilson

5:5   The young have aspirations that never come to pass; the old have reminiscences of what never happened.

H. H. Munro

5:6   Few men of action have been able to make a graceful exit at the appropriate time.

Malcolm Muggeridge

5:7   Children have to learn to live among adults; adults have to learn to live among the angels.

Arnold Haller

5:8   No wise man ever wished to be younger.

Jonathan Swift

5:9   Do not go gentle into that good night. Old age should burn and rave at close of day; Rage, rage against the dying of the light.

Dylan Thomas

5:10 Have you every been out for a late autumn walk in the closing part of the afternoon and suddenly looked up to realise that the leaves have practically all gone? And the sun has set and the day gone before you knew it – and with that a cold wind blows across the landscape? That's retirement.

Stephen Leacock

5:11 Infancy conforms to nobody; all conform to it.

Ralph W. Emerson

5:12 Old men are dangerous; it doesn't matter to them what is going to happen to the world.

George Bernard Shaw

5:13 A boy becomes an adult three years before his parents think he does and about two years after he thinks he does.

Lewis B. Hershey

5:14 If you fulfil your longing to return to your boyhood haunts, you may find that it isn't the haunts you are longing for, but your boyhood.

Mark Twain

5:15 You are worried about seeing him spend his early years in doing nothing. What! Is it nothing to be happy? Nothing to skip, play, and run around all day long? Never in his life will he be so busy again.

J. J. Rousseau

5:16 To youth I have but three words of counsel – work, work, work.

Otto von Bismarck

5:17 So long as little children are allowed to suffer, there is no true love in this world.

Isadora Duncan

5:18 There is no sadder sight than a young pessimist, except perhaps an old optimist.

Mark Twain

5:19 Retirement is the ugliest word in the language.

Ernest Hemingway

5:20 To retire is the beginning of death.

Pablo Casals

5:21 When a man of forty falls in love with a girl of twenty, it isn't her youth he is seeking but his own.

Lenore Coffee

5:22 The old man says to the young man, 'Why are you weeping?'

'I am weeping for my sins,' says the young man.

Months later, they meet again and the young man is still weeping.

'Why are you weeping now?' asks the old man.

'I am weeping because I have nothing to eat.'

'I thought it would come to this,' says the old man.

R. L. Stevenson

5:23 Age does not protect you from love. But love, to some extent, protects you from age.

Jeanne Moreau

5:24 Psychology is singularly adapted for the use of youth, because it has a large vocabulary and is, in its essence, a grand, riotous, complicated, smutty story. It also moves along tramlines and is dressed in uniform. Youth, terrified by the roaring, multitudinous manifestations of life all around it, feels safe with psychology.

James Briodie

5:25 As long as you can still be disappointed, you're still young.

Joyce Cary

5:26 One of the many things that nobody ever tells you about middle age is that it's such a nice change from being young.

Dorothy Fisher

44

5:27 I used to dread getting older because I felt that I wouldn't be able to do all the things I wanted to do, but now that I am older I find I don't want to do them anyway.

Nancy Astor

5:28 The richest I have ever been was when I was a boy and found a five dollar bill. It was the only time in my life I ever had enough money to buy more than I wanted. I guess you can't get richer than that.

Walling Keith

5:29 The burned child dreads the fire – until the next day.

Mark Twain

5:30 The generation gap is the one war in which everybody changes sides.

Cyril Connolly

5:31 The young man who has not wept is a savage, and the older man who will not laugh is a fool.

George Santayana

6: MEN AND WOMEN

6:1   Women who keep their own names are less apt to keep
      their husbands.

Andy Rooney

6:2   The more I see of men, the less I like them. If I could but say
      so of women too, all would be well.

George Gordon

6:3   One hair of a woman can draw more than a hundred pair
      of oxen.

James Howell

6:4   The Christian church says to every bridegroom: 'Through
      this woman you are to explore the whole of womankind.
      If you turn elsewhere, seeking more, you will in fact find
      less.' And this principle applies equally to the bride.

Dominic Cleary

6:5   The formula for a successful marriage is the same as the for-
      mula for a successful motor car manufacturing business
      – stick to the same model.

Henry Ford

6:6   Except for the rare good fortune of finding a congenial
      partner, the least unhappy condition in life is celibacy.

Bernadin de St Pierre

6:7   The credulity of love is most fundamental source of author-
      ity.

Sigmund Freud

6:8   He who is in love with himself has at least this advantage –
      he won't encounter many rivals.

G. C. Lichtenberg

6:9   Of all the delights of this world, man cares most for sexual
      intercourse, yet he has left it out of his heaven.

Mark Twain

6:10 Among all human affection, the human spirit is especially held fast by married love. Consequently, the marriage bond is to be avoided at all costs by those tending to perfection.

Thomas Aquinas

6:11 A happy marriage is the union of two good forgivers.

Robert Quillen

6:12 Women have always been poor, not for two hundred years merely, but from the beginning of time. Women, then, have not had a dog's chance of writing poetry. That is why I have laid so much stress on money and a room of one's own.

Virginia Woolf

6:13 A successful marriage is an edifice that must be rebuilt every day.

André Maurois

6:14 The most important thing a father can do for his children is to love their mother.

Theodore M. Hesburgh

6:15 A married couple are well suited when both partners usually feel the need for a quarrel at the same time.

Jean Rostand

6:16 A hearth is no hearth unless a woman sits by it.

Richard Jefferies

6:17 Who can tell how many of the most original thoughts put forth by male writers belong to a woman by suggestion? If I may judge by my own case, a very large proportion indeed.

John Stuart Mill

6:18 There is no love. Take a couple in love, take them to Ethiopia. They'll eat each other.

Howard Stern

6:19 Unless you love someone nothing makes sense.

e. e. cummings

6:20 The minute you start fiddling around outside the idea of monogamy, nothing satisfies anymore.

Richard Burton

6:21 Marriage begins when the partners recognise their basic incompatabilities.

G. K. Chesterton

6:22 Charm is a sort of bloom on a woman. If you have it, you don't need to have anything else; and if you don't have it, it doesn't much matter what else you have.

J. M. Barrie

6:23 A couple not capable of hating each other are not capable of loving each other either.

Eric Fromm

6:24 Those who have some means think that the most important thing in the world is love. The poor know that it is money.

Gerald Brennan

6.25 What a holler would ensue if people had to pay the minister as much to marry them as they have to pay a lawyer to get them a divorce.

Claire Trevor

6.26 Marriage must incessantly contend with a monster that devours everything – familiarity.

Honoré de Balzac

6:27 There is in every true woman's heart a spark of heavenly fire, which lies dormant in the broad daylight of prosperity, but which kindles up and beams and blazes in the dark hour of adversity.

Washington Irving

6:28 Chains do not hold a marriage together. It is threads, hundred of tiny threads which sew people together through the years. That is what makes a marriage last – more than passion or even sex.

Simone Signoret

6:29 I don't see any reason for marriage when there is divorce.

Catherine Deneuve

6:30 Most men who run down women are running down only a certain woman.

Remy de Gourmont

6:31 This is the age of disposability – the age of the throw-away society. The roads are littered with things people have thrown away; bottles, paper, cans – as well as wives, children and careers. But in our home, if a toaster breaks, we fix it – we don't throw it away. It's the same with a marriage when there are strains. We don't throw it away but see what is wrong and put it right.

Paul Newman

6:32 The first kiss is stolen by the man; the last is begged by the woman.

H. L. Mencken

6:33 Domestic happiness depends on the ability to overlook.

Roy L. Smith

6:34 A fine woman shows her charms to most advantage when she seems most to conceal them. The finest bosom in nature is not so fine as imagination forms.

John Gregory

6:35 Whenever a husband and wife begin to discuss their marriage, they are giving evidence at an inquest.

H. L. Mencken

6:36 Those who devote themselves to the exclusive pursuit of sexual happiness are not apt to find it.

Alfred Gross

49

6:37   Seldom, or perhaps never, does a marriage develop into an individual relationship smoothly and without crises; there is no coming to consciousness without pain.

C. G. Jung

6:38   Absence in love is like water upon fire – a little quickens, but much extinguishes it.

Hannah More

6:39   I have never loved another person the way I loved myself.

Mae West

6:40   We often speak of love when we really should be speaking of the drive to dominate or to master, so as to confirm ourselves as active agents in control of our own destinies and worthy of respect from others.

Thomas Szasz

6:41   Adultery may or may not be sinful, but it is never cheap.

Raymond Postgate

6:42   I love you only on days that end with a 'y'.

Jim Malloy

6:43   There is no female Mozart because there is no female Jack the Ripper.

Camilla Paglia

6:44   A man does not look behind the door unless he has stood there himself.

Henri Dubois

6:45   Marriage is merely sexual blackmail by the female.

Dominic Cleary

6:46   Love is but the discovery of ourselves in others and the delight in that recognition.

Alexander Smith

6:47 God made men stronger but not necessarily more intelligent. He gave women intuition and femininity and, used properly, that combination easily jumbles the brain of any man I ever met.

Farrah Fawcett

6:48 Marriage is an indication of insanity.

Spike Milligan

6:49 There is no one, no one, who loves you like yourself.

Brendan Behan

6:50 Love is what happens to men and women who don't know each other.

Somerset Maugham

6:51 Mammal embryos, deprived of any input of either male or female hormones, always develop as structurally female. Man, in other words, is an afterthought of creation: he is simply a modification of the female.

Deborah Moggach

6:52 Behind almost every woman you ever heard of stands a man who let her down.

Naomi Bliven

6:53 Love ceases to be a pleasure when it ceases to be a secret.

Aphra Behn

6:54 I think being a woman is like being Irish: everyone says you're important and nice, but you take second place all the same.

Iris Murdoch

6:55 It always amuses me to hear a woman describe a man as a 'control freak'. All women are control freaks.

Dominic Cleary

6:56 Prostitutes believe in marriage. It provides them with most of their trade.

Susan Fleming

6:57   No good actor is ever wholly masculine: something, some vocal or physical trait betrays his debt to womankind, the debt which every man owes, but which most of us, out of some primitive animosity, do our best to hide.

Kenneth Tynan

6:58   Where love is concerned, too much is not even enough.

Pierre-Augustin de Beaumarchis

6:59   A man admires a woman not for what she says, but for what she listens to.

George Nathan

6:60   Women fail to understand how much men hate them.

Germaine Greer

6:61   My mission in life is to save feminism from the feminists.

Camilla Paglia

6:62   A fellow who waits to get married until he has enough money, isn't really in love.

Kin Hubbard

6:63   Often the difference between a successful marriage and a mediocre one consists of leaving about three or four things a day unsaid.

Harlan Miller

6:64   Women rule the world. No man has ever done anything that a woman either hasn't allowed him to do or encouraged him to do.

Bob Dylan

6:65   The love that lasts the longest is the love that is never returned.

Somerset Maugham

6:66   To marry happily, pick out a good mother and marry one of her daughters – any one will do.

J. Ogden Armour

6:67   One doesn't have to get anywhere in a marriage. It is not a public conveyance.

Iris Murdoch

6:68   Let us leave pretty women to men without imagination.

Marcel Proust

6:69   Taste is the feminine of genius.

Edward Fitzgerald

6:70   So many persons think that divorce is the panacea for every ill, who find out when they try it, that the remedy is worse than the disease.

Dorothy Dix

6:71   I envy men's naturally raucous sexuality. Male lust is the motor force of civilisation.

Camilla Paglia

6:72   Never marry a man who hates his mother – because he will wind up hating you.

Jill Bennett

6:73   Sometimes it is worth all the disadvantages of marriage just to have one friend in an indifferent world.

Erica Jong

6:74   The one certain way for a woman to hold a man is to leave him for religion.

Muriel Spark

6:75   Love can hope where reason would despair.

George Lyttelton

6:76   Love is the extremely difficult realisation that something other than oneself is real.

Iris Murdoch

6:77   What makes a marriage last is for a man and woman to continue to have things to argue about.

Rex Stout

6:78 Love is like quicksilver in the hand. Leave the fingers open and it stays. Clutch it and it darts away.

Dorothy Parker

6:79 The extreme variational tendency of man expresses itself in a larger percentage of genius, insanity and idiocy; woman remains more nearly normal.

W. I. Thomas

6:80 Absence is to love what wind is to fire. It extinguishes the small, it inflames the great.

Roger de Rabutin

6:81 One doesn't fall in love; one grows into love, and love grows in a person.

Karl Menninger

6:82 As soon as you cannot keep anything from a woman, you love her.

Paul Geraldy

6:83 A man marries one woman to escape from many others, and then chases many others to forget he's married to one.

Helen Rowland

6:84 London is spattered with couples living in sin whose lives are just as dreary as those of the respectably married.

Katharine Whitehorn

6:85 A successful marriage requires falling in love many times, always with the same person.

Mignon McLaughlin

6:86 Once a woman has forgiven a man, she must not reheat his sins for breakfast.

Marlene Dietrich

6:87 No man has ever been taken to hell by a woman unless he already had a ticket in his pocket, or at least had been fooling around with timetables.

Rex Stout

6:88   Inside each man there is a woman. But never was even an Arab lady so well hidden as she.

Paul Valery

6:89   I'd rather have roses on my table than diamonds on my neck.

Emma Goldman

6:90   Find a mate you can groove with. You'll then have an additional brain and sensory organs. The quantity of your experience will be at least doubled and the quality will differ because no two people perceive in exactly the same manner. With a warm perceptive mate you'll be able to freely give and receive love.

Eugene Schoenfeld

6:91   Second marriages collapse at twice the rate of first ones.

Maggie Drummond

6:92   All married couples should learn the art of battle as they should learn the art of making love. Good battle is objective and honest – never vicious and cruel. Good battle is healthy and constructive, and brings to the marriage the principle of equal partnership.

Ann Landers

6:93   A man who has never made a woman angry is a failure in life.

Christopher Morley

6:94   Women are not embarrassed when they buy men's pyjamas, but a man buying a nightgown acts as though he were dealing with a dope peddler.

Jimmy Cannon

6:95   A sound marriage is not based on complete frankness; it is based on sensible reticence.

Morris L. Ernst

6:96 People who are not in love cannot understand how an intelligent man can suffer because of a very ordinary woman. This is like being surprised that someone should be stricken with cholera because of something as insignificant as the common bacillus.

Marcel Proust

6:97 Every night I make love to 25,000 people on stage and go home alone.

Janis Joplin

6:98 A man who is unhappy in love should hang himself not from the nearest tree, but around the neck of the nearest woman.

Jean Renoir

6:99 Women are natural guerrillas. Scheming, we nestle in the enemies bed, avoiding open warfare, watching the options, playing the odds.

Sally Kempton

6:100 Men never learn anything about women, but they have a lot of fun trying.

Olin Miller

6:101 Almost all married people fight, although many are ashamed to admit it. Actually, a marriage in which no quarrelling takes place may well be one that is dead or dying from emotional undernourishment. If you care, you probably fight.

Flora Davis

6:102 The great power of a woman is her theatrical aspect, her mask, her sense of mystery. It is very rarely that you find men who have mystery.

Yves St Laurent

6:103 Love is like a wild rose, beautiful and calm, but willing to draw blood in its defence.

Mark Overby

6:104 Scratch a New Man and you'll find a hypocritical old one. The New Man merely uses his fake sensitivity as a sophisticated form of foreplay.

Mary Mannion

6:105 All the reasons of a man cannot outweigh a single feeling of a woman.

Voltaire

6:106 There are some men in the world who behave with the greatest complaisance, civility and good nature to all ladies whatsoever; except one.

Somerset Maugham

6:107 Love is a fire, but whether it's going to warm your heart or burn your house down, you never can tell.

Joan Crawford

6:108 Love is a perky elf dancing a merry little jig and then suddenly he turns on you with a miniature machine gun.

Matt Groening

6:109 This man – woman thing was a stroke of genius on God's part.

George Bernard Shaw

6:110 You can make divorce as easy as a dog licence, but you can't burn away the sense of shame and waste.

A. Alvarez

6:111 To marry a man out of pity is folly; and, if you think you are going to influence the kind of fellow who has 'never had a chance, poor devil', you are profoundly mistaken. One can influence only the strong characters in life, not the weak; and it is the height of vanity to suppose that you can make an honest man of anyone.

Margot Asquith

6:112 Publication is the male equivalent of childbirth.

Richard Ackland

6:113 Romantic love is a mental illness.

Fran Lebowitz

6:114 True love is like the Lough Ness monster – everybody has heard of it but no one's ever seen it.

Meshack Taylor

6:115 Love is a burnt match skating in a urinal.

Hart Crane

6:116 Assumptions are the termites of relationships.

Henry Winkler

6:117 To fall in love is to create a religion that has a fallible God.

Jorge Luis Borges

6:118 No marriage with a prenuptial agreement has ever lasted.

Desmond Cleary

6:119 Marriage is neither heaven nor hell. It is simply purgatory.

Abraham Lincoln

6:120 If you are a black woman instead of a white man, your life is ten times harder.

Fran Lebowitz

6:121 Women need a reason to be violent, men only need a place.

Jordan Wisenon

6:122 All poets and writers of fiction are adulterers.

Dominic Cleary

6:123 A fish and a bird can fall in love, but where will they build their nest?

Erica Jong

7: Good and Evil

7:1 Forgiveness is the scent the violet leaves on the heel that crushes it.

Mark Twain

7:2 Evil is not an army that besieges a city from outside the walls. It is a native of the city. It is the mutiny of the garrison, the poison in the water, the ashes in the bread.

Charles Morgan

7:3 All sins tend to be addictive and the terminal point of addiction is what is called damnation.

W. H. Auden

7:4 Men never do evil so thoroughly and cheerfully as when they do it for conscience sake.

Blaise Pascal

7:5 It is better to be saved by a lighthouse than by a lifeboat.

Ernest Kunsch

7:6 This downhill path is easy, but there is no turning back.

Christine G. Rossetti

7:7 We don't call it sin today, we call it self-expression.

Mary Stocks

7:8 Error makes the circuit of the globe while Truth is putting on her boots.

Orestes Brownson

7:9 There are a thousand hacking at the branches of evil to one who is striking at the root.

Henry D. Thoreau

7:10 Man is born broken. He lives by mending. The grace of God is glue.

Eugene O'Neill

7:11 You may not be able to change the whole world, but at least you can embarrass the guilty.

Katha Pollitt

7:12 Sin is energy in the wrong channel.

St Augustine

7:13 No man has ever repented of being a Christian on his deathbed.

Henry Ward Beecher

7:14 Every actual state is corrupt. Good men must not obey the laws too well.

Ralph W. Emerson

7:15 Of all possible errors, the worst is being systematically neutral. You can never remain an equal distance between good and evil, because that equal distance is in itself a form of evil.

Jose Descalzo

7:16 The tree of liberty must be refreshed from time to time with the blood of patriots and tyrants. It is its natural manure.

Thomas Jefferson

7:17 If all evil were prevented, much good would be absent from the universe.

Thomas Aquinas

7:18 The line separating good and evil passes not just through states nor between political parties – but right through every human heart.

Alexander Solzhenitsyn

7:19 The first idea that the child must acquire, in order to be actively disciplined, is that of the difference between good and evil; and the task of the educator lies in seeing that the child does not confound good with immobility and evil with activity.

Maria Montessori

7:20 It is much easier to repent of sins we have committed than to repent of those we intend to commit.

Josh Billings

7:21 When you choose the lesser of two evils always remember that it is still an evil.

Max Lerner

7:22 Be virtuous and you will be eccentric.

Mark Twain

7:23 Pornography is a lonely business. It is the sex of the solitary.

Leslie Paul

7:24 We are bound to forgive our enemies but we are not bound to trust them.

Thomas Fuller

7:25 Psycho-analysis is confession without absolution.

G. K. Chesterton

7:26 One leak will sink a ship, and one sin will destroy a sinner.

John Bunyan

7:28 Nothing can be built on regret, but a good life and a happy eternity can be built on repentance.

Arnold Haller

7:29 I never knew anyone to overcome a bad habit gradually.

John R. Mott

7:30 Let no one imagine he has acquired a virtue if he has not been tempted by the contrary vice.

Teresa of Avila

7:31 Evil must not be done that good may come out of it.

Samuel Sewall

7:32 One of the greatest delusions in the world is the hope that the evils of this world can be cured by legislation.

Thomas B. Reed

7:33 All sins have their origin in a sense of inferiority, otherwise called ambition.

C. G. Jung

7:34 Luxury corrupts at once rich and poor, the rich by possession and the poor by covetousness.

J. J. Rousseau

7:35 It may seem quite a distance from divorce American-style to euthanasia Nazi-style, but they both stem from an un-principled ethic which elevates individual desires above the common good.

Gerald Reed

7:36 In reality, hope is the worst of all evils because it prolongs man's torments.

Friedrich Nietzsche

7:37 People don't ever seem to realise that doing what is right is no guarantee against misfortune.

William McFee

7:38 If you haven't any charity in your heart, you have the worst kind of heart trouble.

Bob Hope

7:39 It is the wounded oyster that mends its shell with pearl.
Ralph Waldo Emerson

7:40 To reform a man is tedious and uncertain labour; hanging is the sure work of a minute.

Douglas Jerrold

7:41 You may be sure that when a man begins to call himself a 'realist', he is preparing to do something he is secretly ashamed of doing.

Sydney Harris

7:42 It is easy to have principles when you are rich. The important thing is to have principles when you are poor.

Ray Kroc

7:43 I find that a man with no vices usually has no virtues either.
Abraham Lincoln

7:44 For evil to triumph, all that is needed is for good men to do nothing.
Edmund Burke

7:45 These high places have never been settled by men so they are still innocent. There is not about them any accumulation of evil. Where men have lived a long time, the very stones are saturated in evil memories. Cruelty and suffering remain in the world, and I think the earth cries out under its load of evil.
J. B. Priestley

7:46 All great calamities on land and sea have been traced to inspectors who didn't inspect.
Kin Hubbard

7:47 Never do anything against conscience even if the state demands it.
Albert Einstein

7:48 Forgiveness is man's deepest need and God's highest achievement.
Horace Bushnell

7:49 We have met the enemy and he is us.
Walt Kelly

7:50 Take egotism out and you would castrate all the benefactors.
Ralph Waldo Emerson

7:51 Never fear shadows. They simply mean there's a light shining nearby.
Ruth E. Renkel

7:52 It is easier to stay out than to get out of temptation.
Mark Twain

7:53 If we could all confess our sins to each other we would all laugh at one another for our lack of originality.

Kahil Gibhran

7:54 Necessary evils are still evil.

Thomas Paine

7:55 To do one's duty sounds a rather cold and cheerless business, but somehow in the end it does give one a queer sort of satisfaction.

Somerset Maugham

7:56 What is moral is what you feel good after and what is immoral is what you feel bad after.

Ernest Hemingway

7:57 There is no man so good, who, were he to submit all his thoughts and actions to the law, would not deserve hanging ten times in his life.

Montaigne

7:58 The saints are the sinners who keep on trying.

Robert Louis Stevenson

7:59 The man who has never done any harm will never do any good.

George Bernard Shaw

7:60 The inherent vice of capitalism is the unequal sharing of blessings; the inherent virtue of socialism is the equal sharing of miseries.

Winston Churchill

7:61 Men are not punished for their sins, but by them.

Elbert Hubbard

7:62 Gambling promises the poor what property performs for the rich; that is why the bishops dare not denounce it fundamentally.

George Bernard Shaw

7:63 It is forbidden to kill – unless to the sound of trumpets.

Voltaire

7:64 Poverty and injustice are also the enemies and destroyers of freedom. Until we summon up the resolve to act decisively against them, as we do against the threat of armed aggression, there will be no real peace.

Leonard Cheshire

7:65 Capital punishment is a fundamentally wrong as a cure for crime as charity is wrong as a cure for poverty.

Henry Ford

7:66 If you are afraid of being lonely, don't try to be right.

Jules Renard

7:67 There is one thing about a crop of wild oats – it harvests itself.

Edgar Howe

7:68 Everything that used to be a sin is now a disease.

Bill Maher

7:69 If there is any dishonesty in a man, golf will bring it out.

Paul Gallico

7:70 At what stage in a police inquiry should you bring in a psychologist? Before the crime is committed.

David Carter

7:71 Every reformation must have its victims. You can't expect the fatted calf to share the enthusiasm of the angels over the prodigal's return.

H. H. Munro

7:72 Forgiveness needs to be accepted, as well as offered, before it is complete.

C. S. Lewis

8: WAR AND PEACE

8:1   If you strike a child, take care that you strike it in anger, even at the risk of maiming it for life. A blow in cold blood neither can nor should be forgiven.

George Bernard Shaw

8:2   The use of force alone is but temporary. It may subdue for a moment; but it does not remove the necessity of subduing again: and a nation is not governed, which is perpetually to be conquered.

Edmund Burke

8:3   There never was a good war, nor a bad peace.

Benjamin Franklin

8:4   Non-violence is a flop. The only bigger flop is violence.

Joan Baez

8:5   If sunbeams were weapons of war we would have had solar energy long ago.

George Porter

8:6   Strong men can always afford to be gentle. Only the weak are intent on giving as good as they get.

Elbert Hubbard

8:7   I shall never permit myself so low as to hate any man.

Booker T. Washington

8:8   Every gun that is made, every warship launched, every rocket fired, signifies in the final sense a theft from those who hunger and are not fed, those who are cold and are not clothed.

Dwight D. Eisenhower

8:9   It is well known that firearms go off by themselves if only enough of them are together.

C. G. Jung

8:10 The least pain in our little finger gives us more concern and uneasiness than the destruction of millions of our fellow human beings.

William Hazlitt

8:11 The belief in the possibility of a short decisive war appears to be one of the most ancient and dangerous of human illusions.

Robert Lynd

8:12 You cannot shake hands with a clenched fist.

Indira Gandhi

8:13 War is capitalism with the gloves off.

Tom Stoppard

8:14 My centre is giving way, my right is retreating, situation excellent, I am attacking.

Marshal Foch

8:15 Hatred is a precious liquid, a poison dearer than that of the Borgias – because it is made of our blood, our health, our sleep and two-thirds of our love – we must be stingy with it.

Charles Baudelaire

8:16 No man can put a chain about the ankle of his fellowman without at last finding the other end fastened about his own neck.

Frederick Douglas

8:17 We prefer to lose because of the ability of the opposition rather than the inability of the referee.

Kenny Dalglish

8:18 Nobody ever forgets where he buried the hatchet.

Kin Hubbard

8:19 In peace sons bury their fathers and in war the fathers bury their sons.

Francis Bacon

8:20 The end result of freedom will always be a dictatorship of the masses. Believe me, behind that word 'freedom' demons lurk.

Bernhard Rust

8:21 Only the winners decide what were war crimes.

Gary Wills

8:22 War is common to all and strife in justice, and all things come into being and pass away through strife.

Heraclitus

8:23 No snowflake in the avalanche ever feels responsible.

Stanislaw Lec

8:24 God is usually on the side of big squadrons against the small.

Bussy-Rabutin

8:25 I prefer my people to be loyal out of fear rather than conviction. Convictions can change but fear remains.

Josef Stalin

8:26 Serious sport has nothing to do with fair play. It is bound up with hatred, jealousy, boastfulness, disregard of all rules and sadistic pleasure in witnessing violence; in other words it is war minus the shooting.

George Orwell

8:27 The notion that disarmament can put a stop to war is contradicted by the nearest dogfight.

George Bernard Shaw

8:28 Persecution was at least a sign of personal interest. Tolerance is composed of nine parts of apathy to one of brotherly love.

Frank M. Colby

8:29 Although the world is full of suffering it is also full of the overcoming of suffering.

Helen Keller

8:30 War will exist until that distant day when the conscientious objector enjoys the same reputation and prestige that the warrior does today.

John F. Kennedy

8:31 The enemy is anybody who's going to get you killed, no matter which side he's on.

Joseph Heller

8:32 Appeasers believe that if you keep on throwing steaks to a tiger, the tiger will become a vegetarian.

Heywood Brown

8:33 What do you despise? By this you are truly known.

Frank Herbert

8:34 The nose of the bulldog has been slanted backwards so that he can breathe without letting go.

Winston Churchill

8:35 War will never cease until babies are born into the world with larger brains and smaller adrenal glands.

H. L. Mencken

8:36 Enemies are not those who hate us, but rather those whom we hate.

Dagobert Runes

8:37 Treating your adversary with respect is giving him an advantage to which he is not entitled.

Samuel Johnson

8:38 In order to have good soldiers a nation must always be at war.

Napoleon Bonaparte

8:39 The weakest link in a chain is the most powerful because it can break the chain.

Stanislaw J. Lec

8:40 War is, at first, the hope that one will be better off; next the expectation that the other fellow will be worse off; then, the satisfaction that he isn't any better off; and, finally, the surprise at everyone's being worse off.

Karl Kraus

8:41 Don't hit at all if it is honourably possible to avoid hitting; but *never* hit soft.

Theodore Roosevelt

8:42 Every time you win , you are reborn; when you lose you die a little.

George Allen

8:43 A dead man who never caused others to die seldom rates a statue.

Samuel Butler

8:44 One of the laws of palaentology is that an animal which must protect itself with thick armour is degenerate. It is usually a sign that the species is on the road to extinction.

Gertrude Stein

9: Science and Nature

9:1 After my heart transplant, something in me began to sing. It was more than a resurrection. It was a creation. Adam the second day in the garden: I was going to stay.

A. C. Greene

9:2 I value my garden more for being full of blackbirds than of cherries, and very frankly give them fruit for their songs.

Joseph Addison

9:3 Men of technology are the new and universal priesthood. Their religion is business success; their test of virtue is growth and profit. Their bible is the computer printout; their communion bench is the committee room.

J. K. Galbraith

9:4 I do not know what I may appear to the world, but to myself I seem to have been only a boy playing on the seashore, and diverting myself in now and then finding a smoother pebble or a prettier shell than ordinary, whilst the great ocean of truth lay all undiscovered before me.

Isaac Newton

9:5 Religions die when they are proved to be true. Science is the record of dead religions.

Oscar Wilde

9:6 Science is a cemetery of dead ideas.

Miguel de Unamuno

9:7 When a man wants to murder a tiger, he calls it sport; when a tiger wants to murder him he calls it ferocity.

George Bernard Shaw

9:8 The simplest schoolboy is now familiar with truths for which Archimedes would have given his life.

Ernest Renan

9:9 Architecture is silent music.

J. W. von Goethe

9:10 Really we create nothing. We merely plagiarise Nature.

Jean Baitaillon

9:11 A scientist is not a person who gives the right answers but a person who asks the right questions.

Claude Lévi-Strauss

9:12 An undevout astronomer is mad.

Edward Young

9:13 When the last puritan has disappeared from the earth, the man of science will take his place as a killjoy and we shall be given all the same old advice but for different reasons.

Robert Lynd

9:14 Civilisation is the distance man has placed between himself and his excreta.

Brian Aldiss

9:15 Pollution is nothing but the resources we are not harvesting. We allow them to disperse because we have been ignorant of their value.

R. Buckminster Fuller

9:16 Every formula which expresses a law of nature is a hymn of praise to God.

Maria Mitchell

9:17 Whoever could make two ears of corn or two blades of grass to grow upon a spot of ground where only one grew before, would deserve better of mankind, and do more essential service to his country than the whole race of politicians together.

Jonathan Swift

9:18 I have just bought a computer. I find that wisdom is expiring everywhere under the dead weight of purposeless information.

John Sessions

9:19 A garden is the purest of human pleasure. It is the greatest refreshment to the spirits of man, without which buildings and palaces are but gross handiworks.

Francis Bacon

9:20 Every blade in the field, every leaf in the forest, lays down its life in its season, as beautifully as it was taken up.

Henry D. Thoreau

9:21 The probability of life originating by accident is comparable to the probability of an unabridged dictionary resulting from an explosion in a printing shop.

Edwin Conklin

9:22 The progress of science is strewn, like an ancient desert trail, with the bleached skeletons of discarded theories which once seemed to possess eternal life.

Arthur Koestler

9:23 The universe is not only stranger than we imagine; it is stranger than we can imagine.

J. B. S. Haldene

9:24 Failure in communication isn't always in the transmission. Sometimes the reception can be faulty – migratory words fall dead from exhaustion on the way across the Alps of comprehension.

Christopher Fry

9:25 The eternal silence of the infinite spaces of the Universe frightens me.

Blaise Pascal

9:26 Science without religion is lame; religion without science is blind.

Albert Einstein

9:27 Space flights are merely an escape, a fleeing away from oneself, because it is easier to go to Mars or to the moon than it is to penetrate one's being.

C. G. Jung

9:28 Astronomers of the world co-operate because there is no one nation from which the entire sphere of the sky can be seen. Perhaps there is in that fact a parable for national statesmen, whose political horizons are all too often limited by national horizons.

Adlai Stevenson

9:29 Science does not have a moral dimension. It is like a knife. If you give it to a surgeon or a murderer, each will use it differently.

Werner von Braun

9:30 The doctors treat venereal disease as a medical problem. Lately they have been calling it a social problem. I say it is a moral problem.

Alvie L. McNight

9:31 Ironically, man may be the creature who left as his monument a planet nearly as incapable of sustaining life as its barren neighbours in the dead vacuum of the solar system we are now exploring. Man has an infinite capacity for fouling his environment.

Gaylord Nelson

9:32 It is a mathematical fact that the casting of a pebble from my hand alters the centre of gravity of the universe.

Thomas Carlyle

9:33 Worrying about things that no one else worries about is where insights come from.

Roger Penrose

9:34 Science has 'explained' nothing; the more we know about, the more fantastic the world becomes and the more profound the surrounding darkness.

Aldous Huxley

9:35 The more original a discovery, the more obvious it seems afterwards.

Arthur Koestler

9:36 As cruel a weapon as the caveman's club, the chemical barrage has been hurled against the fabric of life.

Rachel Carson

9:37 The notion that the 'balance of nature' is delicately poised and easily upset is nonsense. Nature is extraordinarily tough and resilient, interlaced with checks and balances, with an astonishing capacity for recovering from disturbances in equilibrium. The formula for survival is not power; it is symbiosis.

Eric Ashby

9:38 Utility is when you have one telephone, luxury is when you have two, opulence is when you have three – and paradise is when you have none.

Doug Larson

9:39 Do always in health what you have often promised to do when you are sick.

Sigmund Freud

9:40 Any sufficiently advanced technology is indistinguishable from magic.

Arthur C. Clarke

9:41 I am a passenger on the spaceship, Earth.

R. Buckminster Fuller

9:42 It was when the more fashionable doctors in Italy, in imitation of the old Romans, despising the work of the hand began to delegate to slaves the manual attentions they deemed necessary for their patients, that the art of medicine went to ruin.

Andreas Vesalius

9:43 In nature there are neither rewards nor punishments – there are consequences.

Robert G. Ingersoll

9:44 Do you believe that the sciences would ever have arisen and become great if there had not beforehand been magicians, alchemists, astrologers and wizards who thirsted and hungered after abscondite and forbidden powers.

Friedrich Nietzsche

9:45 I swear by Apollo the physician, by Asclepius, by Health, by Panacea and by all the gods and goddesses, making them my witnesses, that I will carry out, according to my ability and judgement, this oath and this indenture. To hold my teacher in this art equal to my own parents; to make him partner in my livelihood; when he is in need of money to share mine with him; to consider his family as my own brothers and to teach them this art, if they want to learn it, without fee or indenture; to impart precept, oral instruction, and all other instruction to my own sons, the sons of my teacher, and to indentured pupils who have taken the physician's oath, but to nobody else. I will use treatment to help the sick according to my ability and judgement, but never with a view to injury and wrong-doing. Neither will I administer a poison to anybody when asked to do so, nor will I suggest such a course. Similarly, I will not give a woman a pessary to cause abortion. But I will keep pure and holy both in my life and my art. I will not use the knife, not even, verily, on sufferers from stone but I will give place to such as are craftsmen therein. Into whatsoever houses I enter, I will enter to help the sick, and I will abstain from all intentional wrong-doing and harm, especially from abusing the bodies of man or woman, bond or free, and whatsoever I shall see or hear in the course of my profession, as well as outside my profession in my intercourse with men, if it be what should not be published abroad, I will never divulge holding such things to be holy secret. Now if I carry out this oath, and break it not, may I gain for ever reputation among all men for my life and for my art; but if I transgress it and forswear myself, may the opposite befall me.

Hippocrates

9:46 We have a habit in writing articles published in scientific journals to make the work as finished as possible, to cover up all the tracks, to not worry about and be blind alleys or describe how you had the wrong idea first, and so on. So there isn't any place to publish, in a dignified manner, what you actually did in order to do the work.

Richard Feynman

9:47 When the circuit learns your job, what are you going to do?

Marshall McLuhan

9:48 An apple tree in bloom puts to shame all the men and women that have attempted to dress since the world began.

Henry Ward Beecher

9:49 One does not discover new lands without consenting to lose sight of the shore for a very long time.

André Gide

9:50 Mankind is a catalysing enzyme for the transition from a carbon-based to a silicon-based intelligence.

Gérard Bricogne

9:51 The secret of science is to ask the right question, and it is the choice of problem more than anything else that marks the man of genius in the scientific world.

Henry Tizard

9:52 Any scientist who has ever been in love knows that he may understand everything about sex hormones but the actual experience is something quite different.

Kathleen Lonsdale

9:53 One machine can do the work of fifty ordinary men. No machine can do the work of one extraordinary man.

Elbert Hubbard

9:54 It is a sobering thought to realise that in one second, the sun emits more energy than mankind has used in all the time since civilisation began.

Dominic Cleary

9:55 If you see a formula that extends over a quarter of a page, forget it. It's wrong. Nature isn't that complicated.

Bernal Matthias

9:56 All biological necessities have to be made respectable whether we like it or not.

George Bernard Shaw

9:57 Fresh air is good if you don't take too much of it; most of the achievements and pleasures of life are in bad air.

Oliver W. Holmes

9:58 Science is not to be regarded merely as a storehouse of facts to be used for material purposes, but as one of the great human endeavours to be ranked with arts and religion as the guide and expression of man's fearless quest for truth.

Richard Gregory

9:59 For the scientific, acquisition of knowledge is almost as tedious as the routine acquisition of wealth.

Eric Linklater

9:60 Religions disappear like the mist, empires decay. But the work of scientists lasts for eternity.

Ulugh Beg

9:61 The danger of the past was that men became slaves. The danger of the future is that men may become robots.

Erich Fromm

9:62 Do not free a camel the burden of his hump; you may be freeing him from being a camel.

G. K. Chesterton

9:63 A physicist is just an atom's way of knowing about atoms.

George Wald

9:64 Nobody has ever thought out anything in the shower because it's too fast and too efficient.

Don Herold

9:65 The world began without man and it will end without him.
Claude Lévi-Strauss

9:66 I don't know if there are men on the moon, but if there are, they must be using this earth as their lunatic asylum.
George Bernard Shaw

9:67 No, no, you're not thinking, you're just being logical.
Neils Bohr

9:68 How beautiful the lights of Broadway would appear to someone who could not read.
G. K. Chesterton

9:69 The earth we abuse and the living things we kill with, in the end take their revenge; for in exploiting their presence we are diminishing our future.
Marya Mannes

9:70 My theology briefly is that the universe was dictated but not signed.
Christopher Morley

9:71 Insanity is a perfectly rational adjustment to the insane world.
R. D. Laing

9:72 If a disinfectant smells good, it isn't a good disinfectant.
Edgar Howe

9:73 The Industrial Age had to wait centuries until people in Scotland watched their kettles boil.
A. N. Whitehead

9:74 It is almost impossible systematically to constitute a natural moral law. Nature has no principles. She furnishes us with no reason to believe that human life is to be respected. Nature, in her indifference, makes no distinction between good and evil.
Anatole France

9:75 We have not lost faith, but we have transferred it from God to the medical profession.

George Bernard Shaw

9:76 I finally know what distinguishes me from other beasts: financial worries.

Jules Renard

9:77 The entire universe, with one trifling exception, is composed of others.

John A. Holmes

9:78 A horse never runs so fast as when he has other horses to catch up and outpace.

Ovid

10: MOTHERS AND FATHERS

10:1 Poverty keeps together more homes than it breaks up.

H. H. Munro

10:2 The more people have studied different methods of bringing up children the more they have come to the conclusion that what good mothers and fathers instinctively feel like doing for their babies is the best after all.

Benjamin Spock

10:3 No test tube can breed love and affection. No frozen packet of semen ever read a story to a sleepy child.

Shirley Williams

10:4 Instant availability without continuous presence is probably the best role a mother can play.

Lotte Bailyn

10:5 There is never much trouble in any family where the children hope someday to resemble their parents.

William L. Phelps

10:6 The adolescent is a child who is in the process of receiving from the hands of God, through the intermediary of his parents, personal care of and responsibility for his body, his affections, and his mind.

Michel Quoist

10:7 Inside every pornographer there is an infant screaming for the breast from which it has been torn. Pornography represents an endless and infinitely repeated effort to recapture that breast and the bliss it offered.

Steven Marcus

10:8 The family is the association established by nature for the supply of man's everyday wants.

Aristotle

10:9　In thirty-two years of medical practice we have found that the deprivation of normal parental love is involved in almost every nervous breakdown.

Frank S. Capiro

10:10　A child who has been taught to respect the laws of God will have little difficulty respecting the laws of men.

J. Edgar Hoover

10:11　After I had bathed the children and put them to bed, I thought how deep in human nature was the idea of a family and how false the denial of that idea, as in Plato and in all collective systems, and especially in the present tendency to separate out sensuality and value it apart from procreation. Children are the everlasting new start, life springing up again, joyous and undefiled. I know that my children must make every mistake that I have made, commit the same sins, be tormented by the same passions, as I know that a green shoot pushing up from the earth must ripen and fall back, dead, on to the same earth; yet this does not take away from the wonder and beauty of either children or the spring.

Malcolm Muggeridge

10:12　When my mother died it became sea and islands only. Atlantis had sunk.

C. S. Lewis

10:13　No matter how many communes anybody invents, the family always creeps back.

Margaret Mead

10:14　When you're safe at home you wish you were having an adventure; when you're having an adventure you wish you were safe at home.

Thornton Wilder

10:15　The frightening fact about heredity and environment of children is that parents provide both.

Albert M. Wells

10:16 A boy playing on the deck of a ship in a storm at night was asked by a passenger if he wasn't afraid. 'No,' he replied, 'I am not afraid. My father is captain of the ship'.

Rufus Jones

10:17 Parents are sometimes a bit of a disappointment to their children. They don't fulfil the promise of their early years.

Anthony Powell

10:18 Oh, to be only half as wonderful as my child thought I was when he was small, and only half as stupid as my teenager now thinks I am.

Rebecca Richards

10:19 Most children suffer from too much mother and too little father.

Gloria Steinem

10:20 A child who is allowed to be disrespectful to its parents will not have true respect for anyone.

Billy Graham

10:21 The work will wait while you show your child a rainbow, but the rainbow won't wait while you do the work.

Patricia Clafford

10:22 Children and grandparents are natural allies.

H. J. Brown

10:23 The most important occupation on earth for a woman is to be a real mother to her children. It does not have much glory to it; there is a lot of grit and grime. But there is no greater place of ministry, position or power than that of a mother.

Phil Whisenhunt

10:24 There is no such thing as a non-working mother.

Hester Mundis

10:25 Who has not watched a mother stroke her child's cheek or kiss her child in a certain way and not felt a nervous shudder at the possessive outrage done to a free solitary human soul?

John Cowper Powys

10:26 The understanding of atomic physics is child's play compared with the understanding of child's play.

David Kresch

10:27 I had the total attention of both my parents, and was secure in the knowledge of being loved. My memories of falling asleep at night are to the comfortable sound of my parent's voices, voices which conveyed in their tones the message that these two people loved and trusted each other.

Jill Conway

10:28 There is no more sombre enemy of art than the pram in the hall.

Cyril Connolly

10:29 A pregnant woman's food cravings embody the mother's cannibalistic instincts towards the child.

Darian Leader

10:30 People will not look forward to posterity who never look back to their ancestors.

Edmund Burke

10:31 Sex in the hands of public educators is not a pretty thing.

Kevin Arnold

10:32 There is only one good thing about divorce – you get to sleep with your mother.

Clare Boothe Luce

10:33 The best kind of sex education is life in a loving family.

Rosemary Haughton

10:34 Children may tear up a house, but they never break up a home.

E. C. McKenzie

10:35 Good parents are like turtles – hard on the outside and soft on the inside.

James Hewett

10:36 The only reason I always try to meet and know the parents better is because it helps me to forgive their children.

Louis Johannot

10:37 He that hath wife and children hath given hostages to fortune; for they are impediments to great enterprises, either of virtue or mischief.

Francis Bacon

10:38 Parents have a right to say that no teacher paid by their money shall rob their children of faith in God, and send them back to their homes sceptical, or infidels, or agnostics or atheists.

William J. Bryan

10:39 The best brought-up children are those who have seen their parents as they are. Hypocrisy is not the parents' first duty.

George Bernard Shaw

10:40 Being a parent is tough. If you just want a wonderful creature to love, get a puppy.

Barbara Walters

10:41 Nobody can misunderstand a boy like his own mother.

Norman Douglas

10:42 The family is a court of justice which never shuts down for night or day.

Paul Goodman

10:43 If nature had arranged that husbands and wives should have children alternately, there would never be more than three in a family.

Laurence Housman

10:44 Feminism is a socialist, anti-family, political movement that encourages women to leave their husbands, kill their children, practice witchcraft, destroy capitalism and become lesbians.

Pat Robertson

10:45 Having a baby boy is where the feminist theory collides into reality with a juddering crash.

Dianne Abbott

10:46 One of the oldest human needs is having someone to wonder where you are when you don't come home at night.

Margaret Mead

10:47 The death of a parent makes you ready for the call 'next please'.

Amos Oz

11: CHRISTIANITY AND JESUS

11:1   If it were a crime to be a Christian, would there be enough
       evidence to convict you?

       David Otis Fuller

11:2   Christians do not pass judgement on the personal standing
       of others with God, but they do pass judgement on the
       public effect of a particular witness or testimony.

       G. Aiken Taylor

11:3   If Jesus Christ were to come today, people would not even
       crucify him. They would ask him to dinner, hear what he
       had to say, and make fun of it.

       Thomas Carlyle

11:4   The whole religious complexion of the modern world is due
       to the absence of a lunatic asylum from Jerusalem.

       Havelock Ellis

11:5   Those who talk of the Bible as 'a monument of English
       prose' are merely admiring it as a monument over the
       grave of Christianity.

       T. S. Eliot

11:6   Almost every sect of Christianity is a perversion of its
       essence, to accommodate it to the prejudices of the world.

       William Hazlitt

11:7   The Christian religion is essentially a religion of sensual
       pleasures. Sin is the great attraction; the more one feels
       oneself a sinner, the more Christian one is.

       Novalis

11:8 If there is one part of the Christian message that people have rejected with incomparable obstinacy, it is faith in the equal worth of all souls and races before the Father who is in Heaven.

Francois Mauriac

11:9 That which is always accompanied with effeminate lust – provoking music is doubtless inexpedient and unlawful unto Christians.

William Prynne

11:10 To get to sleep at night I don't count sheep – I talk to the Shepherd.

Harold Taylor

11:11 All my life I have searched for gold at the end of the rainbow until I found it at the foot of the cross.

Dale Evans

11:12 I reject Christianity because it preaches peace on Earth.

Erich Ludendorff

11:13 How else but through a broken heart may the Lord Christ enter in?

Oscar Wilde

11:14 So long as Jesus was misunderstood, He was followed by the crowd. When they came to really understand Him, they crucified Him.

Dan Harman

11:15 The long experience of the church is more likely to lead to correct answers than is the experience of the lone individual.

Elton Trueblood

11:16 As society is now constituted, a literal adherence to the moral precepts scattered throughout the Gospels would mean sudden death.

A. N. Whitehead

11:17 The Christian ideal has not been tried and found wanting. It has been found difficult and left untried.

G. K. Chesterton

11:18 In the early centuries after Christ, Christianity spread because Christians outlived, outloved and outdid the pagans.

Tertullian

11:19 He who shall introduce into public affairs the principles of primitive Christianity will change the face of the world.

Benjamin Franklin

11:20 The Mosaic religion had been a Father religion; Christianity became a Son religion. The old God, the Father, took second place; Christ, the Son, stood in this His stead, just as, in those dark times every son had longed to do.

Sigmund Freud

11:21 Christ was the serpent who deceived Eve.

Peter Ackroyd

11:22 Every great man nowadays has his disciples, and it is always Judas who writes the biography.

Oscar Wilde

11:23 No Christian society has ever known what to do with people who go round taking the Bible literally.

Desmond Cory

11:24 No one ever made more trouble than the 'gentle Jesus meek and mild'.

James M. Gillis

11:25 Where would Christianity be if Jesus had got eight to fifteen years, with time off for good behaviour?

James Donovan

11:26 It wasn't a woman who betrayed Jesus with a kiss.

Catherine Carswell

12: RELIGION AND SECTS

12:1 The ecumenicals are moving ahead with impressive speed because believing little they correspondingly differ about little.

Malcolm Muggeridge

12:2 One psychiatrist has reported that, though he himself does not pretend to be a religious man, he cannot help being impressed by the fact that, in twenty-five years of active practice in New York City, he has never had a patient who really knew how to pray.

William Barclay

12:3 If you are going to have a religion at all, it is better to have it rough – blood and nails and vinegar.

Owen Chadwick

12:4 Religion is the best armour in the world but the worst cloak.

Thomas Fuller

12:5 Superstition is the religion of feeble minds.

Edmund Burke

12:6 Slightly religious people have been inoculated with a mild form of Christianity which prevents them from catching the real thing.

E. S. Jones

12:7 Whenever a man talks loudly against religion, always suspect that it is not his reason, but his passions which have got the better of his creed.

Laurence Sterne

12:8 We have just enough religion to make us hate, but not enough to make us love one another.

Jonathan Swift

12:9   I believe that the Jews have made a contribution to the human condition out of all proportion to their numbers: I believe them to be an immense people. Not only have they supplied the world with two leaders of the stature of Jesus Christ and Karl Marx, but they have even indulged in the luxury of following neither one nor the other.

Peter Ustinov

12:10 The Bible is the greatest medicine chest of humanity.

Heinrich Heine

12:11 The writers against religion, while they oppose every other system, are wisely careful never to set up any of their own.

Edmund Burke

12:12 Man is certainly stark mad: he cannot make a flea, yet he makes gods by the dozen.

Montaigne

12:13 The prodigal son's father did not say to him, 'You stay in the pigsty – we're going to make it a better pigsty.'

Billy Graham

12:14 It is a curious thing that every creed promises a paradise which will be absolutely uninhabitable for anyone of civilised taste.

Evelyn Waugh

12:15 Ancestor-worship is the root of every religion.

Herbert Spencer

12:16 If a surgeon operated on a patient for acute appendicitis and left the appendix in he would be sued for malpractice and fraud. But when a minister preaches to lost men a social gospel which cannot save – well, he may be made a bishop.

L. Nelson Bell

12:17 Men will wrangle for religion, write for it, fight for it, die for it, anything but live for it.

Charles C. Colton

12:18 Theology is the activity of unbelievers.

Karl Popper

12:19 Religion is excellent stuff for keeping common people quiet.

Napoleon Bonaparte

12:20 It is a mistake to assume that God is interested only, or even chiefly, in religion.

William Temple

12:21 The equal toleration of all religions is the same thing as atheism.

Pope Leo XIII

12:22 When I think of all the harm the Bible has done, I despair of ever writing anything to equal it.

Oscar Wilde

12:23 It is not what I don't understand in the Bible that worries me – it's what I do understand.

Mark Twain

12:24 Religion is the fashionable substitute for belief.

Oscar Wilde

12:25: Protestantism is hemiplegic paralysis of Christianity – and of reason.

Friedrich Nietzsche

13: EDUCATION AND LEARNING

13:1 I have never known any trouble that an hour's reading did not improve.

Montesquieu

13:2 The cane and the birch are essentially a fool's implements.
George Bernard Shaw

13:3 If you have knowledge, let others light their candles at it.
Margaret Fuller

13:4 The educated are as superior to the uneducated as the living are to the dead.

Aristotle

13:5 Genius is one per cent inspiration and ninety-nine per cent perspiration.

Thomas Edison

13:6 Creative minds have always been known to survive any kind of bad training.

Anna Freud

13:7 Soap and education are not as sudden as a massacre but they are more deadly in the long run.

Mark Twain

13:8 We never stop investigating. We are never satisfied that we know enough to get by. Every question we answer leads on to another question. This has become the greatest survival trek of our species.

Desmond Morris

13:9 One thing life taught me: if you are interested, you never have to look for new interests. They come to you. When you are genuinely interested in one thing, it will always lead to something else.

Eleanor Roosevelt

13:10 One looks back with appreciation to those brilliant teachers, but with gratitude to those who touched our human feelings. The curriculum is so much necessary raw material, but warmth is the vital element for the growing plant and for the soul of the child.

C. G. Jung

13:11 When a subject becomes totally obsolete we make it a required course.

Peter Drucker

13:12 Education is a state controlled manufactory of echoes.

Norman Douglas

13:13 Those who persist in seeing our primary schools as oases of innocence in which children are kept in ignorance of the need for mental effort or self-control are doing those children a serious disservice.

George Walden

13:14 To teach is to learn twice.

Joseph Joubert

13:15 From the physical features of their work places, no one would ever guess that teachers' work is crucial to the future of the country.

Susan M. Johnson

13:16 I have never let schooling interfere with my education.

Mark Twain

13:17 Only constant repetition will finally succeed in imprinting an idea on the memory of the crowd.

Adolf Hitler

13:18 What we learn with pleasure, we never forget.
Bob Phillips

13:19 When you don't know what you mean, use big words. They often fool little people.
Ernest Hemingway

13:20 Love of books is your pass to the greatest, the purest, and the most perfect pleasure that God has prepared for his creatures. It lasts when all recreations are gone. It will make your hours pleasant to you as long as you live.
Anthony Trollope

13:21 Examination, like interrogation in class, is the refuge of the humdrum teacher who is unable to make his teaching interesting. The main thing in teaching is to give students an interest in their work. No man was ever yet enticed to do this by examinations, but only in spite of them.
Walter McDonald

13:22 Education is what remains when we have forgotten all that we have been taught.
George Savile

13:23 Wherever they burn books they will also, in the end, burn human beings.
Heinrich Heine

13:24 When you educate a man you educate an individual; when you educate a woman you educate a whole family.
Charles D. McIver

13:25 The real struggle is not between east and west, or capitalism and communism, but between education and ignorance.
Martin Buber

13:26 The first gold star a child gets in school for the mere performance of a needful task is its first lesson in graft.
Philip Wylie

13:27 Often praised children become more intelligent than often blamed ones. There's a creative element in praise.

Thomas Dreier

13:28 Genius is recognising the uniqueness in the unimpressive. It is looking at an ugly caterpillar, an ordinary egg and a selfish infant, and seeing a butterfly, an eagle and a saint.

William A. Ward

13:29 A genius! For thirty-seven years I have practised fourteen hours a day, and now they call me a genius!

Pablo Casals

13:30 When I get a little money, I buy books; and if any is left, I buy food and clothes.

Desiderius Erasmus

13:31 There is in our time no well-educated, literate population that is poor; there is no illiterate population that is other than poor.

J. K. Galbraith

13:32 In teaching you cannot see the fruit of a day's work. It is invisible and remains so, maybe for twenty years.

Jacques Barzun

13:33 A child educated only at school is an uneducated child.

George Santayana

13:34 A university is a place where pebbles are polished and diamonds are dimmed.

Robert Ingersoll

13:35 That men do not learn from history is the most important of all lessons that history has to teach.

Aldous Huxley

13:36 Education has produced a vast population able to read but unable to distinguish what is worth reading.

G. M. Trevelyan

13:37 After my two million dollar laboratory was burned down I realised there was great value in disaster. All my mistakes were burned up and thank God I could start anew. Three weeks later I invented the phonograph.

Thomas Edison

13:38 The gains of education are never really lost; books may be burned and cities sacked, but truth, like the yearning for freedom, lives in the hearts of humble men.

Franklin Roosevelt

13:39 Do you see this egg? With it you can overthrow all the schools of theology, all the churches of the earth.

Denis Diderot

13:40 Intellectuals have always opposed the spread of television, just as vociferously as they condemned newspapers in the early part of this century.

John Carey

13:41 Education is simply the soul of a society as it passes from one generation to another.

G. K. Chesterton

13:42 To educate a man in mind, and not in morals, is to educate a menace to society.

Theodore Roosevelt

13:43 Governments never learn. Only people learn.

Milton Friedman

13:44 Education is a private matter between the person and the world of knowledge and experience, and has little to do with school or college.

Lillian Smith

13:45 The investigation of the meaning of words is the beginning of education.

Antisthenes

13:46 A great part of the information I have was acquired by looking up something and finding something else on the way.

Franklin P. Adams

13:47 I will have no intellectual training. Knowledge is ruin
among my young men.

Adolf Hitler

13:48 The illustrator of books is an active fiend who clips with
long sharp shears the tender wings of illusion.

Max Beerbohm

13:49 The one real object of education is to leave a man in the condition of continually asking questions.

Mandel Creighton

13:50 Mediocrity knows nothing higher than itself; but talent
instantly recognises genius.

Arthur Conan Doyle

13:51 Astronomy was born of superstition, eloquence of ambition,
hatred, falsehood and flattery; geometry of avarice, physics of an idle curiosity; and even moral philosophy of
human pride. Thus the arts and sciences owe their birth
to vices.

J. J. Rousseau

13:52 Never miss an opportunity to learn. If you find yourself at
dinner next to a glass eyeball maker, don't make him feel
he's got to talk to you about something he knows nothing about. Get him to tell you how he makes eyeballs.
You're sure to find it enthralling.

Winston Churchill

13:53 The secret of education is to respect the pupil.

Ralph W. Emerson

13:54 Pick adjectives as you would a diamond or a mistress.

Stanley Walker

13:55 If a man empties his purse into his head, no one can take it from him.

Benjamin Franklin

13:56 The things taught in school are not an education but the means to an education.

Ralph W. Emerson

13:57 If I had read as much as other men, I would have been as ignorant as they.

Thomas Hobbes

13:58 There has to be feedback to ascertain the extent to which the message has been understood, believed, assimilated and accepted.

Robert N. McMurray

13:59 If one is master of one thing and understands one thing well, one has at the same time insight into and understanding of many things.

Vincent van Gogh

13:60 The proper time to influence the character of a child is about a hundred years before it is born.

William R. Inge

13:61 Intelligence appears to be the thing that enables a man to get along without education. Education enables a man to get along without the use of his intelligence.

Albert Wiggam

13:62 When the lists go up, much is heard of the candidates' resentment; no one realises with what sadness the examiners did their duty.

Yuan Mei

13:63 Any place where anyone young can learn something useful from someone with experience is an educational institution.

Al Capp

13:64 Some experience of popular lecturing had convinced me that the necessity of making things plain to uninstructed people was one of the very best means of clearing up the obscure corners in one's own mind.

T. H. Huxley

13:65 A judge is a law student who marks his own examination papers.

H. L. Mencken

13:66 I prefer the company of peasants because they have not been educated sufficiently to reason incorrectly.

Montaigne

13:67 The greatest lesson in life is to know that even fools are right sometimes.

Winston Churchill

13:68 How is it that little children are so intelligent and men so stupid? It must be education that does it.

Alexandre Dumas

13:69 Chess is seldom found above the upper-middle class; it's too hard.

Paul Russell

13:70 I have never in my life learned anything from any man who agreed with me.

Dudley Malone

13:71 There are no uninteresting things – just uninterested people.
G. K. Chesterton

13:72 Sixty years ago I knew everything; now I know nothing; education is a progressive discovery of our own ignorance.

Will Durant

13:73 I deem no study good which results in money-making.
Seneca

13:74 Education is an ornament in prosperity and a refuge in adversity.

Aristotle

13:75 None of us got where we are solely by pulling ourselves up by our boot-straps. We got here because somebody – a parent, a teacher, an Ivy League crony or a few nuns – bent down and helped us pick up our boots.

Thurgood Marshall

13:76 Talent is a question of quantity. Talent does not write one page: it writes three hundred.

Jules Renard

13:77 Show me a man who has enjoyed his schooldays and I will show you a bully and a bore.

Robert Morley

13:78 There are two types of genius. Ordinary geniuses do great things, but they leave you room to believe that you could do the same if only you worked hard enough. Then there are magicians, and you have no idea how they do it.

Mark Kac

13:79 The amount of noise which anyone can bear undisturbed stands in inverse proportion to his mental capacity.

Arthur Schopenhauer

13:80 All writing is garbage. People who come out of nowhere to try to put into words any part of what goes on in their mind are pigs.

Antonia Artaud

13:81 Some of the world's greatest feats were accomplished by people not smart enough to know they were impossible.

Doug Larson

13:82 Publication is a self-invasion of privacy.

Marshall McLuhan

13:83 When you have mastered numbers, you will in fact no longer be reading numbers, any more than you read words
when reading books. You will be reading meanings.

Harold Geneen

13:84 Never let me fall into the vulgar mistake of dreaming that I
am persecuted whenever I am contradicted.

Ralph Waldo Emerson

13:85 If you can't write it down, you don't have an idea.

Andy Rooney

13:86 Nothing in education is so astonishing as the amount of
ignorance it accumulates in the form of facts.

Henry Adams

13:87 Genius is perseverance in disguise.

Henry Austin

14: PRAYER AND SUPPLICATION

14:1 The hands that help are holier than the lips that pray.

Robert G. Ingersoll

14:2 Lord, grant that I may always desire more than I can accomplish.

Michelangelo

14:3 Who rises from prayer a better man, his prayer has been answered.

George Meredith

14:4 Prayer is not an old woman's idle amusement. Properly understood and applied, it is the most potent instrument of action.

M. K. Gandhi

14:5 Matthew, Mark, Luke and John,
The bed be blest that I lie on,
Four angels to my bed,
Four angels round my head
One to watch, and one to pray
And two to bear my soul away.

Thomas Ady

14:6 I have lived to thank God that all my prayers have not been answered.

Jean Ingelow

14:7 The wise man in the storm prays to God, not for safety from danger, but for deliverance from the fear.

Ralph W. Emerson

14:8 Forgive, O Lord, my little jokes on Thee, and I'll forgive Thy great big one on me.

Robert Frost

14:9 Never trust somebody who has to change his tone to ask something of the Lord.

Robert Everett

14:10 Have no fear of perfection – you'll never reach it.

Salvador Dali

14:11 Profanity furnishes a relief denied even to prayer.

Mark Twain

14:12 Worry is a prayer for something you don't want.

James M. Miller

14:13 How many of our daydreams would darken into nightmares were there any danger of their coming true.

Henry Thoreau

14:14 The back is fitted to the burden, and I always did pray that if I had work to do, I might be able to do it; and I always was somehow.

Susan Warner

14:15 God, give us grace to accept with serenity the things that cannot be changed, courage to change the things which should be changed, and the wisdom to distinguish the one from the other.

Reinhold Niebuhr

14:16 Don't pray when it rains if you don't pray when the sun shines.

Satchel Paige

14:17 There are only two joys in the world. One is having God answer all your prayers; the other is not receiving the answer to all your prayers.

James Hewett

14:18 To sing is to pray twice.

St Augustine

15: FAITH AND BELIEF

15:1   The centrifugal forces of animal impulse can be balanced only by the centripetal power of religious faith.

David R. Mace

15:2   Give me the benefit of your convictions if you have any, but keep your doubts to yourself for I have enough of my own.

J. W. von Goethe

15:3   If you get through the twilight, you'll live through the night.

Dorothy Parker

15:4   Idealists, foolish enough to throw caution to the winds, have advanced mankind and have enriched the world.

Emma Goldman

15:5   An atheist does not find God for the same reason a thief does not find a policeman. He is not looking for him.

Wendell Baxter

15:6   Selfishness is the only real atheism.

Israel Zangwill

15:7   Doubt is not a pleasant state of mind, but certainty is absurd.

Voltaire

15:8   We can believe what we choose. But we are answerable for what we choose to believe.

John Henry Newman

15:9   A well bred man keeps his beliefs out of his conversation.

André Maurois

15:10   People believe only what they want to believe.

Julius Caesar

15:11 Atheism is just a sort of crutch for those who cannot stand the reality of God.

Tom Stoppard

15:12 Faith may be defined as an illogical belief in the occurrence of the impossible.

H. L. Mencken

15:13 When agnosticism has done its withering work in the mind of man, the mysteries remain as before; all that has been added to them is a settled despair.

Vincent McNabb

15:14 I certainly think that belief in God did give shaping and pattern to life for which I can see no conceivable substitute and to that extent my life is poorer than that of a believer.

Margharita Laski

15:15 Atheists are atheists usually for mean reasons. The meanest of these is that they themselves are so lacking in munificence that they cannot conceive the idea of a divine power.

Patrick White

15:16 I respect faith, but doubt is what gives you an education.

Wilson Mizner

15:17 Nothing is more dangerous than an idea if it's the only one you have.

Benjamin Disraeli

15:18 It is the customary fate of new truths to begin as heresies and to end as superstitions.

Thomas Hurley

15:19 At dusk, three angels come down from the sky to every house. One stands at the door, another sits at the table, and a third watches over the bed. They look after the house and protect it. Neither wolves nor evil spirits can enter the house the whole night long.

Carlo Levi

15:20 There are few so confirmed in atheism, that a pressing danger or the neighbourhood of death will not force to a recognition of the divine power.

Montaigne

15:21 A thing is not necessarily true because a man dies for it.

Oscar Wilde

15:22 The constant assertion of belief is an indication of fear.

Krishnamurti

15:23 Proofs are the last things looked for by a truly religious mind.

George Santayana

15:24 Atheists put on a false courage and alacrity in the midst of their darkness and apprehensions, like children who, when they fear to go in the dark, will sing with fear.

Alexander Pope

15:25 Cynicism is an unpleasant way of saying the truth.

Lillian Hellman

15:26 As far as we can discern, the sole purpose of human existence is to kindle a light in the darkness of mere being.

C. G. Jung

15:27 The three great apostles of practical atheism, that make converts without persecuting, and retain them without preaching are wealth, health and power.

Charles C. Colton

15:28 Truth never damages a cause that is just.

Mahatma Gandhi

15:29 That all men are equal is a proposition to which, at ordinary times, no sane individual has ever given his assent.

Aldous Huxley

15:30 It is easier to fight for one's principles than to live up for them.

Alfred Adler

15:31 You can preach a better sermon with your life than with your lips.

Oliver Goldsmith

15:32 Sometimes I think we are alone in the Universe. Sometimes I think we are not alone. In either case, the thought is quite staggering.

R. Buckminster Fuller

15:33 A lie can be halfway around the world before the truth has got its boots on.

James Callaghan

15:34 Religions are kept alive by heresies, which are really sudden explosions of faith.

Gerald Brennan

15:35 Some men see things as they are and ask why. Others dream things that never were and ask why not.

George Bernard Shaw

15:36 Don't be an agnostic – be something.

Robert Frost

15:37 Chance is a word that does not make sense. Nothing happens without a cause.

Voltaire

15:38 Like all weak men, he laid exaggerated stress on not changing one's mind.

Somerset Maugham

15:39 When an argument is over, how many weighty reasons does a man recollect which his heat and violence made him utterly forget?

Eustace Budgell

15:40 Never try to reason the prejudice out of a man; it was not reasoned into him and cannot be reasoned out.

Samuel Johnson

15:41 The only thing that makes life possible is permanent intolerable uncertainty; not knowing what comes next.

Ursula le Guin

15:42 Oh what a goodly outside falsehood hath.

William J. Gaynor

15:43 The man who cannot believe his senses, and the man who
cannot believe anything else, are both insane.

G. K. Chesterton

15:44 The most common of all follies is to believe passionately in
the palpably not true. It is the chief occupation of mankind.

H. L. Mencken

15:45 To know what you prefer, instead of humbly saying Amen
to what the world tells you you ought to prefer, is to have
kept your soul alive.

Robert Louis Stevenson

15:46 When a thing is funny, search for a hidden truth.

George Bernard Shaw

15:47 People need hard times and oppression to develop psychic
muscles.

Frank Herbert

15:48 Freedom consists not in doing what we like, but in having
the right to do what we ought.

Pope John Paul II

15:49 If you are scared to go to the brink, you are lost.

John Foster Dulles

15:50 The truth is not always the same as the majority decision.

Pope John Paul II

15:51 Something unpleasant is coming when men are anxious to
tell the truth.

Benjamin Disraeli

15:52 A great deal of intelligence can be invested in ignorance when the need for illusion is deep.

Saul Bellow

15:53 Our quaint metaphysical opinions, in an hour of anguish, are like playthings by the bedside of a child deathly sick.

Samuel Taylor Coleridge

15:54 It is easier to give an apology than to receive permission.

Clifford Stoll

15:55 To die for an idea is to set rather a high price upon conjecture.

Anatole France

15:56 Getting out of bed in the morning is an act of false confidence.

Jules Feiffer

15:57 It is only about things that do not interest one that one can give a really unbiased opinion, which is no doubt the reason why an unbiased opinion is always valueless.

Oscar Wilde

16: PHILOSOPHY AND THOUGHT

16:1 A little philosophy inclineth men's minds to atheism; but depth in philosophy bringeth men's minds about to religion.

Francis Bacon

16:2 Analysing humour is like cutting a skylark's throat to see what makes it sing.

Bryan McMahon

16:3 There is no such thing as free will. The mind is induced to wish this or that by some cause and that cause is determined by another cause and so on back to infinity.

Spinoza

16:4 In view of the widespread silliness of the majority of mankind, a widespread belief is more likely to be foolish than sensible.

Bertrand Russell

16:5 Disinterested intellectual curiosity is the life blood of real civilisation.

G. M. Trevelyan

16:6 Do not be ashamed to say what you are not ashamed to think.

Michel de Montaigne

16:7 Do not labour under the common illusion that you make things better by talking about them.

Rose MacAulay

16:8 A great many people think they are thinking when they are merely rearranging their prejudices.

William James

16:9　He that lives upon hope will die fasting.

Benjamin Franklin

16:10　Paradox is just truth standing on its head to attract attention.

G. K. Chesterton

16:11　Genius consists in solving the problems of everyday life.

Edward de Bono

16:12　Let us never allow ourselves to depart from truth; it is the beginning of all iniquity.

Elizabeth Hamilton

16:13　The mind is an iceberg. It floats with only a tenth of its bulk above water.

Sigmund Freud

16:14　Very few people think more than three or four times a year. I owe my fame to the fact that I think once or twice a week.

George Bernard Shaw

16:15　There is no idea so powerful as the one whose time has come. And, on the other hand, all the intelligence in the world is of no avail against a piece of stupidity which is thought to be in fashion.

Bernard Levin

16:16　In my experience, the worst thing you can do to an important problem is to discuss it.

Simon Gray

16:17　Any philosophy that can be put in a nutshell belongs there.

Sydney J. Harris

16:18　Three passions, simple but overwhelmingly strong, have governed my life: the longing for love, the search for knowledge, and unbearable pity for the suffering of mankind.

Bertrand Russell

16:19 The misfortunes hardest to bear are those which never come.

Bob Phillips

16:20 What was once thought can never be unthought.

Friedrich Durrenmath

16:21 We are all of us sentenced to solitary confinement inside our own skins for life.

Tennessee E. Williams

16:22 The wise learn from tragedy; the foolish merely repeat it.

Michael Novak

16:23 It is not miserable to be blind; it is miserable to be incapable of enduring blindness.

John Milton

16:24 Facts do not cease to exist because they are ignored.

Aldous Huxley

16:25 Posterity will some day laugh at the foolishness of modern materialistic philosophy. The more I study nature, the more I am amazed at the Creator.

Louis Pasteur

16:26 Scientists are explorers – philosophers are merely tourists.

Richard Feynman

16:27 On earth there is nothing great but man; in man there is nothing great but mind.

William Hamilton

16:28 There is no record in human history of a happy philosopher.

H. L. Mencken

16:29 We have found a strange footprint on the shores of the unknown. We have devised profound theories, one after the other, to account for its origin. At last we have succeeded in reconstructing the creature that made the footprint. And lo! It is our own.

Arthur Eddington

16:30 People demand freedom of speech as a compensation for the freedom of thought which they seldom use.

Sören Kierkegaard

16:31 All good things are cheap, all bad things very dear.

Henry Thoreau

16:32 There are few people, even among the calmest thinkers, who have not occasionally been startled into a vague yet thrilling half-credence in the supernatural, by coincidences of so seemingly marvellous a character that, as mere coincidences, the intellect has been unable to receive them.

Edgar Allan Poe

16:33 If I knew what I was so anxious about, I wouldn't be so anxious.

Mignon McLaughlin

16:34 Miracles sometimes occur, but one has to work terribly hard for them.

Chaim Weizmann

16:35 Dogma does not mean the absence of thought, but the end of thought.

G. K. Chesterton

16:36 The course of true anything never does run smooth.

Samuel Butler

16:37 When we remember we are all mad, the mysteries disappear and life stands explained.

Mark Twain

16:38 It is a profoundly erroneous truism, repeated by all copy books and by eminent people when they are making speeches, that we should cultivate the habit of thinking of what we are doing. The precise opposite is the case. Civilisation advances by extending the number of important operations which we can perform without thinking about them.

A. N. Whitehead

16:39 One of my favourite philosophical tenets is that people will agree with you only if they already agree with you. You do not change people's minds.

Frank Zappa

16:40 Loyalty to petrified opinion never yet broke a chain or freed a human soul.

Mark Twain

16:41 A hidden connection is stronger than an obvious one.

Heraclitus

16:42 A cynic is a man who knows the price of everything and the value of nothing.

Oscar Wilde

16:43 Ignorance is the necessary condition of life itself. If we knew everything, we could not endure existence for a single hour.

Anatole France

16:44 To be conscious that you are ignorant is a great step to knowledge.

Benjamin Disraeli

16:45 There is only one way under high heaven to get the best of an argument – and that is to avoid it.

Dale Carnegie

16:46 There is nothing so powerful as an idea whose time has come.

Victor Hugo

16:47 We have not got the same reverent feeling for the rainbow that a savage has. We have lost as much as we have gained by prying into the matter.

Mark Twain

16:48 Going to the moon isn't very far; the greatest distance we have to cover still lies within us.

Charles de Gaulle

16:49 A dwarf on giant's shoulders sees further of the two.

George Herbert

16:50 Philosophy is a route of many roads, leading from nothing to nowhere.

Ambrose Bierce

16:51 Women do none of the philosophising, and have all the philosophy.

Don Herold

16:52 It is easy to build a philosophy – it doesn't have to run.

Charles Kettering

16:53 It is a most mortifying reflection for a man to consider what he has done, compared to what he might have done.

Samuel Johnson

16:54 The secret isolated joy of the thinker is that a hundred years after he is dead and forgotten, men who never heard of him will be moving to the measure of his thought.

Oliver W. Holmes

16:55 Just remember, we're all in this alone.

Lily Tomlin

16:56 You must never regret what might have been. The past that did not happen is as hidden from us as the future we cannot yet see.

Richard Stern

16:57 A good catchword can obscure analysis for fifty years.

Wendell Wilkie

16:58 If you cannot catch a bird of paradise, better take a wet hen.

Nikita Khrushchev

16:59 The truth is always the perfect alibi.

W. R. Burnett

16:60 When one door closes another door opens; but we so often look so long and so regretfully upon the closed door, that we do not see the ones which open for us.

Alexander Graham Bell

16:61 Once the people begin to reason, all is lost.

Voltaire

16:62 Yes and no are the oldest and simplest words, but they require the most thought.

Pythagoras

16:63 Don't wait for the last judgement. It takes place every day.

Albert Camus

16:64 Men who deserve monuments do not need them.

Gene Fowler

16:65 Be careful what you pretend to be because you are what you pretend to be.

Kurt Vonnegut

16:66 I have always known that at last I would take this road – but I did not know yesterday that it would be today.

K. Rexroth

16:67 Nothing lasts forever: not even your troubles.

Arnold Glasow

16:68 Be careful what you set your heart upon, for it will be surely be yours.

James Baldwin

16:69 Decide promptly, but never give your reasons. Your decisions may be right but your reasons are sure to be wrong.

Lord Mansfield

16:70 You cannot be anything if you want to be everything.

Solomon Schechter

16:71 If we want a thing badly enough, we can make it happen.

Dorothy L. Sayers

17: POLITICS AND POWER

17:1 The Nazis came for the Communists and I didn't speak up because I was not a Communist. They came for the Jews and I didn't speak up for I was not a Jew. They came for the trade unionists and I didn't speak up because I was not a trade unionist. They came for the Catholics and I was a Protestant so I didn't speak up. Then they came for me and by that time there was no one left so speak up.

Martin Niemöller

17:2 No character, however upright, is a match for constantly reiterated attacks, however false.

Alexander Hamilton

17:3 The kingly office is entitled to no respect. It was originally procured by highwayman's methods; it remains a perpetuated crime, can never be anything but the symbol of a crime. It is no more entitled to respect than is the flag of a pirate.

Mark Twain

17:4 You can afford the luxuries of the left wing – save the whales, stop uranium mining, grants to the arts, increasing pensions – only if you are a prosperous right wing country. A dictator should step in and abolish the left wing and handouts. Then after four or five years the country will be back on the rails and we can bring back all the benevolent left-wing services.

Paul Hogan

17:5 Socialism will work in only two places; in heaven where it's not needed, and in hell where they already have it. Capitalism is the unequal distribution of wealth. Socialism is the equal distribution of poverty. Communism is nothing but socialism with a gun to your head.

Winston Churchill

17:6 Russian Communism is the illegitimate child of Karl Marx and Catherine the Great.

Clement Atlee

17:7 Democracy is the worst form of government there is, except for every other that has been tried.

Winston Churchill

17:8 Russia has two Generals in whom she can confide – Generals Janvier and Fevrier.

Emperor Nicholas I

17:9 Bad governments are elected by good citizens who do not vote.

George J. Nathan

17:10 Freedom is the right to tell people what they don't want to hear.

George Orwell

17:11 The dirty work at political conventions is almost always done in the grim hours between midnight and dawn. Hangmen and politicians work best when the human spirit is at its lowest ebb.

Russell Baker

17:12 Monarchy is only the string which ties the robber's bundle.

Percy B. Shelley

17:13 It is dangerous to be right in matters on which the established authorities are wrong.

Voltaire

17:14 Universal suffrage is the most monstrous and iniquitous of tyrannies – because the force of numbers is most brutal, having neither courage nor talent.

Paul Bourget

17:15 Foreign aid is taxing poor people in rich countries for the benefit of rich people in poor countries.

Bernard Rosenberg

17:16 The most tolerant definition of an honest politician is one whose political actions are not dictated by a desire to increase his own income.

Bertrand Russell

17:17 In general, the art of government consists in taking as much money as possible from one party of the citizens to give to the other.

Voltaire

17:18 If in a country the only news which is published is good news, then be sure that in that country the jails are full of good men.

Patrick Moynihan

17:19 I would much rather have men ask why I have no statue than why I have one.

Marcus Cato

17:20 The oppressed are allowed once every few years to decide which particular representatives of the oppressing class are to represent and repress them.

Karl Marx

17:21 *Mein Kampf* is the only honest book any politician has ever written.

W. H. Auden

17:22 Aristocracies, as a rule, all the world over, consist, and have always consisted, of barbaric conquerors or their descendants, who remain to the last, on the average of instances, at a lower grade of civilisation and morals than the democracy they live among.

Grant Allen

17:23 The only good government is a bad one in a hell of a fright.

Joyce Cary

17:24 For estimating the intelligence of a ruler, look at the men he has around him.

Nicholas Machiavelli

17:25 The minority is always right.

Henrik Ibsen

17:26 When statesmen forsake their own private consciences for the sake of their public duties, they lead their country by a short route to chaos.

Thomas More

17:27 The king has been very good to me. He promoted me from a simple maid to be a marchioness. Then he raised me to be a queen. Now he will raise me to be a martyr.

Anne Boleyn

17:28 Facts show that politically independent trade unions do not exist anywhere. There have never been any. Experience and theory say that there will never be any.

Leon Trotsky

17:29 America is the only place where they lock up the jury every night and let the prisoner go home.

Harry Hershfield

17:30 Trade unions are islands of anarchy in a sea of chaos.

Aneurin Bevan

17:31 Corruption is the most infallible symptom of constitutional liberty.

Edward Gibbon

17:32 It is international sport that helps kick the world downhill. Started by foolish athletes who thought it would promote understanding, it is supported today by the desire for political prestige and by the interests involved in gate money. It is completely harmful.

E. M. Forster

17:33 Government has no other end but the preservation of property.

John Locke

17:34 Destiny is a tyrant's authority for crime, and a fool's excuse for failure.

Ambrose Bierce

17:35 I prefer the sign *No Entrance* to the sign that says *No Exit*.
Stanislaw J. Lec

17:36 You cannot be a politican and remain honest.

Louis Howe

17:37 Patriotism is the willingness to kill and be killed for trivial reasons.

Bertrand Russell

17:38 Public relations is the art of arranging the truth so that people will like you.

Alan Harrington

17:39 Democracy encourages the majority to decide things about which the majority is blissfully ignorant.

John Simon

17:40 Socialism is nothing but the capitalism of the lower classes.
Oswald Spengler

17:41 No country without an atomic bomb can properly consider itself independent.

Charles de Gaulle

17:42 I wait until the last available minute and then I always vote with the losers. Because, my friend, the winners never remember and the losers never forget.

Thomas H. Kean

17:43 Communism has done a lot for us. In fact our souls contain exactly the contrary of what they wanted. They wanted us not to believe in God and our churches are full. They wanted us to be materialistic and incapable of sacrifice: we are anti-materialistic, capable of sacrifice. They wanted us to be afraid of the tanks, of the guns, and instead we don't fear them at all.

Lech Walesa

17:44 You took my freedom away a long time ago and you can't give it back because you haven't got it yourself.

Alexander Solzhenitsyn

17:45 Liberty is the only thing you cannot have unless you give it to others.

William White

17:46 Queen Victoria was like a great paperweight that for half a century sat upon men's minds, and when she was removed their ideas began to blow about all over the place haphazardly.

H. G. Wells

17:47 All terrorists, at the invitation of the Government, end up with drinks at the Dorchester.

Hugh Gaitskell

17:48 In a hierarchy every employee tends to rise to his level of incompetence. In time, every post tends to be occupied by an employee who is incompetent to carry out its duties. Work is accomplished by those employees who have not yet reached their level of incompetence.

Laurence J. Peter

17:49 Whenever you find yourself on the side of the majority, it is time to pause and reflect.

Mark Twain

17:50 What is the point of having a vote if there is nobody worth voting for?

Shirley MacLaine

17:51 Rebels are those unlucky persons who, when things have come to violence, have the misfortune to be of the weaker party.

Adam Smith

17:52 A free society is a place where it's safe to be unpopular.

Adlai Stevenson

17:53 A democracy is a government in the hands of men of low birth, no property and vulgar employments.

Aristotle

17:54 The right to do something does not mean that doing it is right.

William Safire

17:55 There seem to be but three ways for a nation to acquire wealth. The first is by war, as the Romans did, in plundering their conquered neighbours. This is robbery. The second by commerce, which is generally cheating. The third by agriculture, the only honest way, wherein man receives a real increase of the seed thrown into the ground, in a kind of continual miracle, wrought by the hand of God in his favour, as a reward for his innocent life and his virtuous industry.

Benjamin Franklin

17:56 Money is the most important thing in the world; and all sound and successful personal and national morality should have this fact for its basis.

George Bernard Shaw

17:57 The great nations have always acted like gangsters and the small nations like prostitutes.

Stanley Kubrick

17:58 Every revolution evaporates and leaves behind only the slime of a new bureaucracy.

Franz Kafka

17:59 Tyrants seldom need excuses.

Edmund Burke

17:60 Patriotism is the virtue of the vicious.

Oscar Wilde

17:61 With the pride of the artist, you must blow against the walls of every power that exists, the small trumpet of your defiance.

Norman Mailer

18: Feelings and Emotions

18:1 I will show you a love potion without drug or herb or any witch's spell; if you wish to be loved, love.

Seneca

18:2 When people are bored, it is primarily with their own selves that they are bored.

Eric Hoffer

18:3 There are two tragedies in life. One is to lose your heart's desire. The other is to gain it.

George Bernard Shaw

18:4 Envy is a coal that comes hissing hot from hell.

Philip J. Bailey

18:5 When a man or woman loves to brood over a sorrow and takes care to keep it green in their memory, you may be sure it is no longer a pain to them.

Jerome K. Jerome

18:6 A lifetime of happiness; no man alive could bear it; it would be hell on earth.

George Bernard Shaw

18:7 Freedom is when one hears the bell at 7 o'clock in the morning and knows it is the milkman and not the Gestapo.

Georges Bidault

18:8 The moment you cheat for the sake of beauty, you know you are an artist.

Max Jacob

18:9 The greatest happiness you can have is knowing you do not necessarily need happiness.

William Saroyan

18:10 The human soul needs actual beauty more than bread.

D. H. Lawrence

18:11 Never forget what a man says to you when he is angry.

Henry Ward Beecher

18:12 Remember that the most beautiful things in the world are also the most useless; peacocks and lilies for instance.

John Ruskin

18:13 Listen to music religiously as if it were the last strain you might hear.

Henry D. Thoreau

18:14 We are never happy: we can only remember that we were so once.

Alexander Smith

18:15 Good music is that which penetrates the ear with facility and quits the memory with difficulty.

Thomas Beecham

18:16 Not in doing what you like best, but in liking what you do, is the secret of happiness.

J. M. Barrie

18:17 The whole conviction of my life now rests upon the belief that loneliness, far from being a rare and curious pheno-menon, peculiar to myself and a few other solitary men, is the central and inevitable fact of human existence.

Thomas Wolfe

18:18 Happiness is like a butterfly which, when pursued, stays always just beyond your grasp – but which, if you sit down quietly, may alight upon you.

Nathaniel Hawthorne

18:19 Jealousy signifies a weakness in the capacity to love, a lack of self-confidence.

Ernest Jones

18:20 A man that does not know how to be angry does not know how to be good.

Henry Ward Beecher

18:21 Song is the licensed medium for bawling in public things too silly or sacred to be uttered in ordinary speech.

Oliver Herford

18:22 Music and rhythm find their way into the secret places of the soul.

Plato

18:23 'I can forgive, but I cannot forget' is only another way of saying 'I cannot forgive'.

Henry Ward Beecher

18:24 There are two insults which no human will endure: the assertion that he hasn't got a sense of humour, and the doubly impertinent suggestion that he has never known trouble.

Sinclair Lewis

18:25 This could be such a beautiful world.

Rosalind Welcher

18:26 The less secure a man is, the more likely he is to have extreme prejudices.

Clint Eastwood

18:27 When somebody says 'I hope you won't mind my telling you this', it's pretty certain that you will.

Sylvia Bremner

18:28 The search for happiness is one of the chief sources of unhappiness.

Eric Hoffer

18:29 Pain nourishes courage. You cannot be brave if you've only had wonderful things happen to you.

Mary Tyler Moore

18:30 When you are playing, do not be concerned about who is listening to you. Always play as though a master were listening to you.

Zoltán Kodály

18:31 Happiness is not a place – it is a direction.

Bill Sands

18:32 The three things which people seek as the key to happiness are money, fame and sensual pleasure. But wherever the key lies, it is most certainly not in any of these.

Spinoza

18:33 I have never yet seen anyone whose desire to build up his moral desire was as strong as sexual desire.

Confucius

18:34 Today's non-stop music, piped from shuddering plastic boxes, debauches the senses of one of its sacred pleasures. Music should be a voluptuous treat, like a deep hot bath, not a continuous shriek in the plumbing.

Laurie Lee

18:35 We have no more right to consume happiness without producing it than to consume wealth without producing it.

George Bernard Shaw

18:36 Worry is interest paid on trouble before it becomes due.

William R. Inge

18:37 Avarice is the sphincter of the heart.

Matthew Green

18:38 Happiness lies not in having what you want but in wanting what you have.

Hartley Howard

18:39 There is no such thing as an unmusical person.

Hans W. Henze

18:40 Music is no different from opium. Music affects the human mind in a way that makes people think of nothing but music and sensual matters. Opium produces one kind of sensitivity and lack of energy, music another kind. A young person who spends most of his time with music is distracted from the serious and important affairs in life; he can get used to it in the same way as he can to drugs. Music is a treason to the country, a treason to our youth, and we should cut out all this music and replace it with something instructive.

Ayatollah Khomeini

18:41 Whoever is spared personal pain must feel himself called to help in diminishing the pain of others.

Albert Schweitzer

18:42 Artists are the eyes for other people.

Henry Moore

18:43 Love is the key to the entire therapeutic programme of the modern psychiatric hospital.

Karl A. Menninger

18:44 Happiness is an imaginary condition formerly often attributed by the living to the dead, now usually attributed by adults to children and by children to adults.

Thomas Szasz

18:45 Composing music is like making love to the future.

Lukas Foss

18:46 Boredom is a sickness the cure for which is work; pleasure is only a palliative.

Le Duc de Lévis

18:47 Annual income twenty pounds, annual expenditure nineteen pounds nineteen and sixpence, result happiness. Annual income twenty pounds, annual expenditure twenty pounds and sixpence, result misery.

Charles Dickens

18:48 The deepest need of man is the need to overcome his separateness, to leave the prison of his aloneness.

Erick Fromm

18:49 A sip is the most that mortals are permitted from any goblet of delight.

Amos B. Alcott

18:50 There is no such thing as pure pleasure; some anxiety always goes with it.

Ovid

18:51 A man will give up almost anything except his suffering.

John Cleese

18:52 Try to regard your states of mind as visits to places. Now I am in the angry place or the melancholy place or the misunderstood-by-everybody place. The point is, if you do this you don't identify yourself with these states of mind: they are not you.

J. B. Priestley

18:53 Fear is the parent of cruelty.

James A. Froude

18:54 Broken hearts die slowly.

Thomas Campbell

18:55 Humour is mankind's greatest blessing.

Mark Twain

18:56 Music is a splendid art but a sad profession.

Jim Pietsch

18:57 I prefer counselling rich people to poor people. Rich people already know that a million dollars isn't going to make you happy.

Alan Monk

18:58 A man's wealth can be measured in terms of what he can do without.

R. A. Freeman

18:59 Courage is the art of being the only one who knows you are scared to death.

Peter Eldin

18:60 The crown of literature is poetry. It is its end and aim. It is the most sublime activity of the human mind. It is the achievement of beauty and delicacy. The writer of prose can only step aside when the poet passes.

Somerset Maugham

18:61 You can discover what your enemy fears most by observing the means he uses to frighten you.

Eric Hoffer

18:62 Happiness is never in our power and pleasure is. I doubt whether anyone who has tasted joy would ever, if both were in his power, exchange it for all the pleasure in the world.

C. S. Lewis

18:63 Happiness is not attained through self-gratification but through fidelity to a worthy purpose.

Helen Keller

18:64 You must first have a lot of patience to learn to have patience.

Stanislaw J. Lec

18:65 Bad artists always admire each other's work.

Oscar Wilde

18:66 The way to love anything is to realise that it might be lost.

G. K. Chesterton

18:67 The woods are lovely, dark and deep
But I have promises to keep,
And miles to go before I sleep
And miles to go before I sleep.

Robert Frost

18:68 All art is a kind of subconscious madness expressed in terms of sanity.

George Nathan

18:69 Next to enjoying ourselves, the next greatest pleasure consists in preventing others from enjoying themselves, or, more generally, in the acquisition of power.

Bertrand Russell

18:70 Happiness is not something you experience; it's something you remember.

Oscar Levant

18:71 Revenge is a delicious fruit that you must leave to ripen.

Emile Gaboriau

18:72 I stretched out my hand to Beauty and Love and they thrust it away.

W. C. Fields

18:73 Jealousy is the great preservative of family life and marital faithfulness. Jealousy is the inseparable companion of love and its intensity is the pure gauge of love's strength.

William McDougal

18:74 I never get angry, even at social injustice. Why should I expend energy in anger that I can expend in love?

Mother Teresa

18:75 The man who lets himself be bored is even more contemptible than the bore.

Samuel Butler

18:76 When power leads man to arrogance, poetry reminds him of his limitations. When power narrows the area of man's concern, poetry reminds him of the richness and diversity of his existence. When power corrupts, poetry cleanses.

John F. Kennedy.

18:77 Peace and happiness begin, geographically, where garlic is used in cooking.

Marcel Boulestin

18:78 The world belongs to the enthusiast who keeps cool.

William McFee

18:79 When the fast bowler hits you, don't rub the sore place – you don't want to let him know you are hurt. Just grin and bear it.

Roy Hattersley

18:80 Cynicism is just despair dressed up as sophistication.

David Puttnam

18:81 Atonality was the great barrier reef on which modern music shattered, as the stream of consciousness was the torpedo that sank the novel and abstraction the anaesthetic that put painting to sleep.

Bernard Levin

18:82 Grief is a species of idleness.

Samuel Johnson

18:83 Inflation is the one form of taxation that can be imposed without legislation.

Milton Friedman

18:84 Conceit is God's gift to little men.

Bruce Barton

18:85 If I were a dictator I should make it compulsory for every member of the population between the ages of four and eighty to listen to Mozart for at least one quarter of an hour daily for the coming five years.

Thomas Beecham

18:86 Without art, the crudeness of reality would make the world unbearable.

George Bernard Shaw

18:87 The function of music is to release us from the tyranny of conscious thought.

Thomas Beecham

18:88 It is better to be quotable than honest.

Tom Stoppard

18:89 There is no happiness except in the realisation that we have accomplished something.

Henry Ford

18:90 Suffering is the main condition of the artistic experience.

Samuel Beckett

18:91 Show me a thoroughly satisfied man – and I will show you a failure.

Thomas Edison

18:92 As long as I have a want, I have a reason for living. Satisfaction is death.

George Bernard Shaw

19: FRIENDSHIP AND SOCIETY

19:1 While there is a lower class I am in it; while there is a criminal element I am of it; while there is a soul in prison, I am not free.

Eugene V. Debs

19:2 I realise that patriotism is not enough. I must have no hatred or bitterness towards anyone.

Edith Cavell

19:3 It is easier to forgive an enemy than to forgive a friend.

William Blake

19.4 Friendship is every bit as sacred and eternal as marriage.

Katherine Mansfield

19.5 The chain of friendship, however bright, does not stand the attrition of constant close contact.

Walter Scott

19.6 Friendship is love without wings.

George Gordon

19.7 Friends are fictions founded on some momentary experience.

Ralph Waldo Emerson

19.8 I believe sexuality is the basis of all friendship.

Jean Cocteau

19.9 I must have first place or none. I cannot bear a slight from those I love.

Mary Wollstonecraft

19.10 Friendship will not stand the strain of very much good advice.

Robert Lynd

20: MISCELLANEOUS

20:1   We owe to the Middle Ages the two worst inventions of humanity – romantic love and gunpowder.

André Maurois

20:2   Advertising is the greatest art form of the twentieth century.

Marshal McLuhan

20:3   It is terrible to speak well and be wrong.

Sophocles

20:4   The real art of conversation is not only to say the right thing in the right place but to leave unsaid the wrong thing at the tempting moment.

Dorothy Nevill

20:5   Ordinary riches can be stolen; real riches cannot. In your soul are infinitely precious things that cannot be taken from you.

Oscar Wilde

20:6   A first class soup is vastly superior to a second class painting.

Paul Gauguin

20:7   The earth provides enough for every man's need but not for every man's greed.

Mahatma Gandhi

20:8   Literature was born on the day when a boy came out of the woods crying 'wolf, wolf' and there was no wolf behind him.

Vladimir Nabokov

20:9   Success is never luck, but a mysterious power of the successful.

Giuseppe Verdi

20:10 Professional critics are those who brush the clothes of their betters.

Francis Bacon

20:11 What is called a high standard of living consists in considerable measure in arrangements for avoiding muscular energy, increasing sensual pleasure, and enhancing calorie intake beyond any conceivable nutritional requirement. Nonetheless, the belief that increased production is a worthy social goal is very nearly absolute.

J. K. Galbraith

20:12 When you read a biography, remember that the truth is never fit for publication.

George Bernard Shaw

20:13 There are two hundred million poor in the world who would gladly take the vow of poverty if they could eat, dress and have a home like myself and many of those who profess the vow of poverty.

Fulton J. Sheen

20:14 Go into the street and give one man a lecture on morality, and another a shilling, and see which will respect you most.

Samuel Johnson

20:15 Actors are the opposite of people.

Tom Stoppard

20:16 Advertising is the rattling of a stick inside a swill bucket.

George Orwell

20:17 A ship is safe in the harbour, but that is not what ships are for.

Albert J. Nimeth

20:18 There is a limit at which forbearance ceases to be a virtue.

Edmund Burke

20:19 Never extend your hand further than you can withdraw it.
Seamus MacManus

20:20 Luck and destiny are the excuses of the world's failures.
Henry Ford

20:21 One must be poor to know the luxury of giving.
George Evans

20:22 I write when I am inspired and I see to it that I am inspired at nine o'clock every morning.
Peter de Vries

20:23 A magazine is dead unless each issue offends at least a fifth of its subscribers.
Charles Peguy

20:24 It is his reasonable conversation which mostly frightens us in a madman.
Anatole France

20:25 Mendings are honourable; rags are abominable.
Dominic Cleary

20:26 Like a piece of ice on a hot stove the poem must ride on its own melting.
Robert Frost

20:27 There are no shortcuts to anywhere that's worth going to.
Beverley Sills

20:28 In the fight between you and the world, back the world.
Franz Kafka

20:29 Only birds sing for nothing.
Enrico Caruso

20:30 Never claim as a right what you can ask as a favour.
J. Churton Collins

20:31 The rule is jam yesterday and jam tomorrow, but never jam today.

Lewis Carroll

20:32 There is no evidence that there is any advantage in belonging to a pure race. The purest races now in existence are the Pygmies, the Hottentots, and the Australian aborigines. The Tasmanians, who were probably even purer, are extinct. They were not the bearers of a brilliant culture.

Bertrand Russell

20:33 There are no stains on the pages of tomorrow.

Grady B. Wilson

20:34 The right to be heard does not automatically include the right to be taken seriously.

Hubert Humphrey

20:35 People have no special rights because they belong to one race or another. The word *human* defines all rights.

José Martí

20:36 Every builder of every home should be compelled to attach his name, in some permanent but inconspicuous way to that house – for better or for worse.

Andy Rooney

20:37 Man needs difficulties; they are necessary for health.

C. G. Jung

20:38 I hang on to my prejudices; they are the testicles of my mind.

Eric Hoffer

20:39 Mañana does not mean tomorrow. It means not today.

Fred Hoctor

20:40 Delay is the deadliest form of denial.

C. N. Parkinson

20:41 No good story is quite true.

Leslie Stephen

20:42 All fighters are prostitutes and all promoters are pimps.

Larry Holmes

20:43 A play should give you something to think about. When I see a play and understand it the first time, then I know it can't be much good.

T. S. Eliot

20:44 Traveller, there is no path; paths are made by walking.

Antonio Machado

20:45 In America, sport is the opium of the masses.

Russell Baker

20:46 Amateur musicians practise until they get it right; professional musicians practise until they cannot get it wrong.

Harold Craxton

20:47 Don't ever slam a door; you might want to go back.

Don Herold

20:48 The cure for anything is salt water – sweat, tears, or the sea.

Joseph Conrad

20:49 It is bad enough to know the past; it would be intolerable to know the future.

Somerset Maugham

20:50 We should all be obliged to appear before a board every five years, and justify our existence to its satisfaction on pain of liquidation.

George Bernard Shaw

20:51 The darkest hour has only sixty minutes.

Morris Mandel

20:52 We Irish are a very perverse complex people. We are banking heavily that God has a sense of humour.

Jim Murray

20:53 History is largely the glorification of the iniquities of the triumphant.

Paul Eldridge

20:54 As long as people will pay admission to a theatre to see a naked body rather than a naked mind, the drama will languish.

George Bernard Shaw

20:55 Fame is something which must be won; honour is something which must not be lost.

Arthur Schopenhauer

20:56 All conservatism is based upon the idea that if you leave things alone, you leave them as they are. But you do not. If you leave a thing alone you leave it to a torrent of change.

G. K. Chesterton

20:57 Inflation is the world's most successful thief.

Carl Pearson

20:58 You can run an office without a boss, but not without secretaries.

Jane Fonda

20:59 Never saw off the branch you are on, unless you are being hanged from it.

Stanislaw J. Lec

20:60 In all of recorded history there has not been one economist who has had to worry about where the next meal would come from.

Peter F. Drucker

20:61 Dark circles under the eyes are not made with a compass.

Don Herold

20:62 The well dressed man is he whose clothes you never notice.

Somerset Maugham

20:63 Wrinkles should merely indicate where smiles have been.
Mark Twain

20:64 At the age of ninety-five, I still practise the cello six hours a day, because I think I'm making progress.
Pablo Casals

20:65 An actor is a sculptor who carves in snow.
Edwin Booth

20:66 If a law were passed giving six months in jail to every writer of a first book, only the good ones would do it.
Bertrand Russell

20:67 We are confronted with insurmountable opportunities.
Walt Kelly

20:68 A madman is not the man who has lost his reason. A madman is the man who has lost everything except his reason.
G. K. Chesterton

20:69 Poverty is a virtue greatly overrated by those who no longer practise it.
Barnaby Keeney

20:70 If you cannot afford the expensive model, don't buy anything.
Andy Rooney

20:71 In the final analysis fame is not important. No matter how great a man is, the size of his funeral usually depends on the weather.
Rosemary Clooney

20:72 If you have an important point to make, don't try to be subtle or clever. Use a pile driver. Hit the point once. Then come back and hit it again. Then hit it a third time – a tremendous whack.
Winston Churchill

20:73 Great persecutors are recruited among martyrs whose heads haven't been cut off.

E. M. Cioran

20:74 I have seen gross intolerance shown in support of toleration.

Samuel Taylor Coleridge

20:75 Free verse is like free love: it is a contradiction in terms.

G. K. Chesterton

20:76 There are moments when everything goes well – don't be frightened, it won't last.

Jules Renard

20:77 The only time you cannot afford to fail is the last time you try.

Charles Kettering

20:78 There is only one proof of ability – results.

Harry Banks

20:79 Kodak sells film but they don't advertise film. They advertise memories.

Theodore Levitt

20:80 Never demean yourself by talking back to a critic, never. Write those letters to the editor in your head, but don't put them on paper.

Truman Capote

20:81 All rising to great place is by a winding stair.

Francis Bacon

20:82 For a fine performance only two things are absolutely necessary: the maximum of virility coupled with the maximum of delicacy.

Thomas Beecham

20:83 Nothing is so fatiguing as the eternal hanging on of an uncompleted task.

William James

INDEX

Bertin, Eugene P. 3:33
Bevan, Aneurin 17:30
Bibesco, Elizabeth 3:118
Bidault, Georges 18:7
Bierce, Ambrose 16:50, 17:34
Billings, Josh 1:41, 7:20
Binyon, Laurence 1:4
Bitsberger, Donald 1:14
Blair, Junior 1:52
Blake, William 19:3
Bliven, Naomi 6:52
Bohr, Neils 9:67
Baileau, Nicholas 3:16
Bok, Curtis 3:34
Boleyn, Anne 17:27
Bonaparte, Napoleon 3:75,
    8:38, 12:19
Bonhoeffer, Dietrich 2:64
Booth, Edwin 20:65
Borges, Jorge Luis 6:117
Boulestin, Marcel 18:77
Bourget, Paul 17:14
Bradford, John 2:28
Bradstreet, Anne 3:2
Bramah, Ernest 3:125
Bremner, Sylvia 18:27
Brennan, Gerald 3:135, 6:24,
    15:34
Bricogne, Gérard 9:50
Briodie, James 5:24
Bronowski, Jacob 4:18
Brooks, Louise 3:94
Brown, Heywood 8:32
Brown, H. J. 10:22
Browne, Thomas 1:55
Brownson, Orestes 7:8
Bryan, William J. 10:38
Buber, Martin 13:25
Budgell, Eustace 15:39
Bunyan, John 7:26

Burke, Edmund 7:44, 8:2,
    10:30, 12:5,
12:11, 17:59, 20:18
Burnett, W. R. 16:59
Burton, Richard 4:26, 6:20
Bushnell, Horace 7:48
Butler, Samuel 1:58, 2:10, 3:88,
    8:43, 16:36, 18:75

Caesar, Julius 15:10
Callaghan, James 15:33
Campbell, Thomas 18:54
Camus, Albert 16:63
Cannon, Jimmy 6:94
Capiro, Frank S. 10:9
Capote, Truman 20:80
Capp, Al 13:63
Carey, John 13:40
Carnegie, Andrew 3:66
Carnegie, Dale 3:129, 3:133,
    16:45
Carlyle, Thomas 1:34, 3:38,
    9:32, 11:3
Carretto, Carlo 2:38
Carroll, Lewis 20:31
Carson Rachel 9:36
Carswell, Catherine 11:26
Carter, David 7:75
Caruso, Enrico 20:29
Carver, George 3:139
Cary, Joyce 5:25, 17:23
Casals, Pablo 5:20, 13:29, 20:64
Cato, Marcus 3:15, 3:120, 17:19
Cavanaugh, Brian 2:40
Cavell, Edith 19:2
Céline, Louis 1:22
Chadwick, Owen 12:3
Chamfort, Nicolas 1:38
Cheshire, Leonard 7:64
Chesterfield, Lord 3:37, 4:22

146

Dreier, Thomas 13:27
Drummond, Maggie 6:91
Drucker, Peter 13:11, 20:60
Dubois, Henri 6:44
Dulles, John Foster 15:49
Dumas, Alexandre 13:68
Duncan, Isadora 5:17
Durant, Will 13:72
Durrenmath, Friedrich 16:20
Dylan, Bob 6:64

Eastwood, Clint 18:26
Eddington, Arthur 16:29
Edison, Thomas 3:44, 4:32,
    13:5, 13:37, 18:91
Edwards, Jonathan 3:3
Einstein, Albert 2:1, 7:47, 9:26
Eisenhower, Dwight D. 8:8
Eldin, Peter 18:59
Eldridge, Paul 1:60, 20:53
Eliot, T. S. 3:146, 11:5, 20:43
Ellis, Havelock 11:4
Emerson, Ralph W. 2:34, 5:11,
    7:14, 7:39, 7:50, 13:53,
    13:56, 13:84, 14:7, 19:7
Epicurus 1:50
Erasmus, Desiderius 13:30
Ernst, Morris L. 6:95
Evans, Dale 11:11
Evans, George 20:21
Everett, John W. 2:4
Everett, Robert 14:9
Exum, Jack 3:113

Fawcett, Farrah 6:47
Feiffer, Jules, 15:56
Feynman, Richard 9:46, 16:26
Fields, W. C. 18:72
Fisher, Dorothy 5:26
Fitzgerald, Edward 6:69

Fitzgerald F. Scott 3:109, 4:27
Fleming, Susan 6:56
Foch, Marshal 8:14
Fonda, Jane 20:58
Ford, Henry 6:5, 7:65, 18:89,
    20:20
Forster, E. M. 17:32
Forte, Charles 3:69
Fosdick, Harry E. 3:36
Foss, Lukas 18:45
Fowler, Gene, 16:64
France, Anatole 2:33, 9:74,
    15:55, 16:43, 20:24
Franklin, Benjamin 3:57, 3:111,
    8:3, 11:19, 13:55, 16:9, 17:55
Freeman, R. A. 18:58
Freire, Paulo 3:24
Freud, Anna 13:6
Freud, Sigmund 6:7, 9:39,
    11:20, 16:13
Friedman, Milton 13:43, 18:83
Fromm, Eric, 6:23, 9:61, 18:48
Frost, Robert 14:8, 15:36, 18:67,
    20:26
Froude, James A. 3:71, 18:53
Fry, Christopher 9:24
Fuller, David Otis 11:1
Fuller, Margaret 13:3
Fuller, R. Buckminster 9:15,
    9:41, 15:32
Fuller, Thomas 1:19, 2:45, 3:81,
    3:102, 7:24, 12:4

Gaborian, Emile 18:71
Gaitskell, Hugh 17:47
Galbraith, J. K. 1:48, 9:3, 13:31,
    20:11
Gallico, Paul 7:74
Gandhi, Indira 8:12
Gandhi, Mahatma 2:55, 2:62,

147

Landers, Ann 4:11, 6:92
Lardner, Ring 4:4
Larson, Doug 9:38, 13:81
Laski, Margharita 15:14
Laurence, D. H. 18:10
Laver, Rod 3:35
Leacock, Stephen 5:9
Leader, Darian 10:29
Lebowitz, Fran 4:28, 6:113,
    6:120
Lec, Stanislaw 2:13, 8:23, 8:39,
    17:35, 18:64, 20:59
Le Grúin, Ursula 15:41
Lee, Laurie 18:34
Lee, Robert E. 4:29
Lerner, Max 7:21
Leo XIII, Pope 12:21
Lewin, Michael Z. 3:124
Lewis, C. S. 1:8, 2:7, 2:12, 2:47,
    2:48, 2:61, 7:72, 10:12, 18:62
Lewis, Sinclair 18:24
Levenson, Sam 3:19
Levant, Oscar 18:70
Levi, Carlo 15:19
Levin, Bernard 16:15, 18:81
Levins, Rosario 2:63
Levi-Strauss, Claude 9:11, 9:65
Levitt, Theodore 20:79
Lichtenberg, G. C. 1:46, 3:92,
    3:97, 3:108, 6:8
Lincoln, Abraham 3:121, 6:119,
    7:43
Linklater, Eric 9:59
Livy 3:18
Lloyd-George, David 3:112
Locke, John 17:33
Lonsdale, Kathleen 9:52
Lowe, Rob 3:30
Lowell, James 3:99
Luce, Clare Boothe 10:32

Ludendorff, Erich 11:12
Lynch, Peter 3:98
Lynd, Robert 8:11, 9:13, 19:10
Lyttleton, George 6:75

Mace, David R. 15:1
Machado, Antonio 20:44
Machiavelli, Nicholas 17:24
Maeterlinck, Maurice 1:15
Maher, Bill 7:68
Mailer, Norman 17:61
Malloy, Jim 6:42
Malone, Dudley 13:70
Mandel, Moris 20:51
Mann, Thomas 1:16
Mannes, Marya 9:69
Mannion, Mary 6:104
Mansfield, Katherine 19:4
Mansfield, Lord 16:69
Marcus, Steven 10:7
Marquis, Don 1:43
Marshall, Thurgood 13:75
Marti, José 20:35
Marx, Karl 17:20
Mason, Helen 4:21
Mastroianni, Colleen 1:20
Matthias, Bernal 9:55
Maugham, Somerset 1:56,
    3:138, 6:50, 6:65, 6:106,
    7:55, 15:38, 18:60, 20:49,
    20:62
Mauriac, Francois 11:8
Maurois, André 6:13, 15:9 20:1
Mead, Margaret 10:32, 10:46
Mei, Yuan 13:62
Mencken, H. L. 2:26, 3:12,
    3:141, 6:32, 6:35, 8:35,
    13:65, 15:12, 15:44 16:28
Menninger, Karl 6:81, 18:43
Meredith, George 14:3

Ostler, William 2:57, 3:132
Overby, Mark 6:103
Ovid, 3:78, 9:78, 18:50
Oz, Amos 10:47

Paglia, Camilla 3:115, 6:43,
    6:61, 6:71
Paige, Satchel, 14:16
Paine, Thomas 7:54
Parker, Dorothy, 6:78, 15:3
Parkinson, C. N. 20:40
Pascal, Blaise 3:68, 7:4, 9:25
Pasteur, Louis 16:25
Paul, Leslie 7:23
Pavlova, Anna 2:32
Payne, Raymond 3:84
Pearson, Carl 20:57
Peguy, Charles 20:23
Pelli, Caesar 3:42
Penrose, Roger 9:33
Peter, Laurence J. 17:48
Peters, Ellis 2:54
Phelps, William L. 10:5
Phillips, Bob 3:29, 13:18, 16:19
Pickford, Mary 3:52
Pietsch, Jim 18:56
Plato 18:22
Poe, Edgar Allan 16:32
Pollit, Katha 7:11
Pope, Alexander 2:8, 15:24
Popper, Karl 2:16, 12:18
Porter, George 8:5
Postgate, Raymond 6:41
Powell, Anthony 10:17
Powys, John Cooper 10:25
Priestley, J. B. 1:9, 7:45, 18:52
Proust, Marcel 6:68, 6:96
Prynne, William 11:9
Puttnam, David 18:80
Pythagoras, 16:62

Quillin, Robert 6:11
Quoist, Michel 10:6

Rabutin, Bussy 8:24
Ramuz, Charles 1:18
Reed, Gerald 7:35
Reed, Thomas B. 7:32
Renan, Ernest 9:8
Renard, Jules 7:66, 9:76, 13:76,
    20:76
Renkel, Ruth E. 7:51
Renoir, Jean 6:98
Rexroth, K. 16:66
Rice, Elmer 4:25
Rice-Davies, Marilyn 1:13
Richards, Rebecca 10:18
Richler, Mordecai 1:59
Risley, C. A. 2:30
Roberta-Burdett, Joyce 4:3
Robertson, Pat 10:44
Roche, John P. 3:64
Rooney, Andy 6:1, 13:85, 20:36,
    20:70
Roosevelt, Eleanor 3:72, 3:73,
    13:9
Roosevelt, Franklin 13:38
Roosevelt, Theodore 8:41,
    13:42
Rosen, Richard 1:27
Rosenberg, Bernard 17:15
Rossetti, Christine G. 7:6
Rostand, Jean 6:15
Rousseau, J. J. 3:25, 5:15, 7:34,
    13:51
Rowland, Helen 6:83
Runes, Dagobert 8:36
Russell, Bertrand 3:55, 3:58,
    16:4, 16:18, 17:16, 17:37,
    18:69, 20:32, 20:66
Russell, Paul 13:69

Ruskin, John 3:62, 18:12
Rust, Bernhard 8:20

Safire, William 17:54
Sands, Bill 18:31
Santayana, George 3:59, 5:31, 13:33, 15:23
Saroyan, William 18:9
Satir, Virginia 3:93
Savile, George 13:22
Saville, Horatio 4:16
Sayers, Dorothy L. 16:71
Schecter, Solomon 16:70
Schoenfeld, Eugene 6:90
Schopenhauer, Arthur 1:51, 13:79, 20:55
Schuller, Robert 3:10
Schweitzer, Albert 18:41
Scott, Walter 19:5
Seneca 13:73, 18:1
Sessions, John 9:18
Sewall, Samuel 7:31
Shaw, George Bernard 2:22, 2:59, 3:96, 5:12, 6:109, 7:59, 7:62, 8:1, 8:27, 9:7, 9:56, 9:66, 9:75, 10:39, 13:2, 15:35, 15:46, 16:14, 17:56, 18:3, 18:6 18:35, 18:86, 18:92, 20:12, 20:50, 20:54
Sheen, Fulton J. 20:13
Shelley, Percy B. 17:12
Shipp, Tom 4:8
Signoret, Simone 6:28
Sills, Beverley 20:27
Simon, John 17:39
Simon, Neil 4:17
Smith, Adam 17:51
Smith, Alexander 6:46, 18:14
Smith, Fred 3:61
Smith, Lillian 13:44

Smith, Logan P. 2:2, 3:80, 3:128
Smith, Roy L. 6:33
Solzhenitsyn, Alexander 7:18, 17:44
Sophocles 20:3
Spark, Muriel 6:74
Spencer, Herbert 12:15
Spengler, Oswald 17:40
Spinoza 16:3, 18:32
Spock, Benjamin 10:2
Stalin, Josef 8:25
Steffens, Lincoln 2:43
Stein, Gertrude 8:44
Steinem, Gloria 10:19
Stern, Gil 3:117
Stern, Howard 6:18
Stern, Richard 16:56
Sterne, Laurence 12:7
Stephen, Leslie 20:41
Stevenson, Adlai 9:28, 17:52
Stevenson, Robert Louis 3:13, 5:22, 7:58, 15:45
St Laurent, Yves 6:102
Stocks, Mary 7:7
Stoll, Clifford 15:54
Stoppard, Tom 8:13, 15:11, 18:88, 20:15
Stout, Rex 3:126, 6:77, 6:87
Stowe, Harriet Beecher 2:18, 3:45
Swift, Jonathan 5:8, 9:17, 12:8
Swope, Herbert B. 3:23
Szasz, Thomas 6:40, 18:44

Taylor, G. Aiken 11:2
Taylor, Harold 11:10
Taylor, Meshack 6:114
Temple, William 12:20
Teresa, Mother 2:51, 3:31, 3:83, 5:1, 18:74

MORE INTERESTING BOOKS

SOMETHING UNDERSTOOD
A SPIRITUAL ANTHOLOGY

EDITED BY SEÁN DUNNE

This anthology contains a rich selection of writings on many aspects of spirituality. They include God, pain, prayer, love, loss, joy and silence. Drawing on the great traditions of Christian spirituality, Seán Dunne has assembled pieces by dozens of writers, among them Thomas Merton, Simone Weil, Teresa of Avila, John Henry Newman, and Dietrich Bonhoeffer. He has also chosen from the work of creative writers such as Patrick Kavanagh, John McGahern, Kate O'Brien and George Herbert. With a wide selection of material that ranges from just a few lines to many pages, *Something Understood* is a perfect source for reflection on aspects of spirituality that have been the concern of men and women through the centuries.

THE SPIRIT OF
TONY DE MELLO

A HANDBOOK OF MEDITATION EXERCISES

JOHN CALLANAN, SJ

This book captures the essence and spirit of Tony de Mello. He was a great teacher. Some said he was a dangerous one. He constantly challenged himself, the world within which he lived and those he came into contact with. For some this element of challenge was both unsettling and confusing. Tony said that our security does not lie in thoughts or ideas no matter how profound. Neither does it lie in traditions – no matter how hallowed. Security can only reside in an attitude of mind and a readiness to reflect deeply, thus subjecting any and every belief to rigorous questioning.

So Tony urged people to question, question. Questions often make us uncomfortable. They do, however, force us to reflect and thus ensure our growth.

John Callanan has started the book with an opening chapter on the basics of prayer. Then he moves on to try and give a flavour of the ideas and themes which gave so much zest and life to Tony de Mello's presentations. The exercises in this book are based on the prayer-style which Tony himself developed during his retreats.

PETER CALVEY
HERMIT

DAVID TORKINGTON

This a fast-flowing and fascinating story of a young priest in search of holiness and of the hermit who helps him. The principles of Christian Spirituality are pinpointed with a ruthless accuracy that challenges the integrity of the reader, and dares him to abandon himself to the only One who can radically make him new. The author not only shows how prayer is the principal means of doing this, but he details a 'Blue Print' for prayer for the beginner, and outlines and explains the most ancient Christian prayer tradition, while maintaining the same compelling style throughout.

PETER CALVEY
PROPHET

DAVID TORKINGTON

This book is first and foremost a brilliant exposition of the inner meaning of prayer and of the profound truths that underlie the spiritual life. Here at last is a voice that speaks with authority and consummate clarity amidst so much contemporary confusion, of the only One who makes all things new and of how to receive Him.

STORIES FOR PREACHERS

JAMES A FEEHAN

Part of the challenge facing the preacher today is getting the message across Sunday after Sunday. Only too often he faces a television saturated congregation which seems either unwilling or unable to listen to him. If he doesn't actually hear the click of the switch-off, then one glance at the glazed looks in the pews should convince him that the pulpit may well be losing the battle with the box.

Stories for Preachers is written from a conviction that the massive boredom in our churches today stems from the fact that the average Sunday worshipper is incapable of sustained listening for more than a few minutes. If it can't be said in six to seven minutes it can't be got across at all. The short homily calls for long and painstaking preparation and needs to be illuminated by apt and imaginative illustrations.

The preacher today is faced with the challenge of bringing the reality of Christ to a people bewildered by the fantasies of the media – and *Stories for Preachers* is an attempt to meet this challenge.

PREACHING IN STORIES

JAMES A. FEEHAN

Preaching in Stories is a plea for creative preaching, a return to the storytelling process in breaking the bread of God's word. Drawing on almost four decades of preaching Fr Feehan builds his case on the interaction of three stories in the Sunday homily – the story or faith experience of the preacher, the story of God and the story of the listeners.

As well as stories galore there are some fine examples of creative writing as in the story of the Four Friends where the author sees the miracle of the healing of the paralysed man through the eyes of four different people, pictured in his imagination as the four friends who let the sick man down through the roof.

BODY-MIND MEDITATION
A GATEWAY TO SPIRITUALITY

LOUIS HUGHES, OP

You can take this book as your guide for a fascinating journey that need not take you beyond your own hall door. For it is an inward journey, and it will take you no further than God who, for those who want him as a friend, lives within. On the way to God-awareness, you will be invited to experience deep relaxation of body and mind.

Body-Mind Meditation can help you become a more integrated balanced person. It is an especially helpful approach to meditation if the pace of life is too fast for you, or if you find yourself frequently tense or exhausted.